THE MERCIFUL
HUMILITY OF GOD

THE MERCIFUL HUMILITY OF GOD

The 2019 Lent Book

Jane Williams

BLOOMSBURY CONTINUUM

LONDON · NEW YORK · OXFORD · NEW DELHI · SYDNEY

BLOOMSBURY CONTINUUM
Bloomsbury Publishing Plc
50 Bedford Square, London, WC1B 3DP, UK

BLOOMSBURY, BLOOMSBURY CONTINUUM and the Diana logo are
trademarks of Bloomsbury Publishing Plc

First published in Great Britain 2018

A catalogue record for this book is available from the British Library

Library of Congress Cataloguing-in-Publication data has been applied for

ISBN: PB: 978-1-4729-5481-7; ePDF: 978-1-4729-5483-1;
ePub: 978-1-4729-5482-4

2 4 6 8 10 9 7 5 3 1

Typeset by Newgen KnowledgeWorks Pvt. Ltd., Chennai, India
Printed and bound in Great Britain by CPI Group (UK) Ltd, Croydon CR0 4YY

To find out more about our authors and books visit www.bloomsbury.com
and sign up for our newsletters

CONTENTS

INTRODUCTION

Lent begins with a reminder of our mortality. The Ash Wednesday custom is to use ashes to mark the forehead with the sign of the Cross. As the ashes are daubed, the priest says: 'Remember that you are dust, and to dust you will return.' That sombre note stays with us for the season of Lent, as we strip away illusions of power and control and face the reality that we are mortal, dependent and ephemeral. The season is one for serious reflection on ourselves, our lives, our priorities. But it is not the purpose of Lent to plunge us all into gloom and depression, but rather to allow a new light into our self-reflection during its 40 days. The light we use to illuminate these reflections is the light of Jesus Christ. In Lent, we are preparing ourselves for the holiest season of the Christian year – Holy Week and Easter, when we see the heart of God laid bare. What we actually see, of course, is a human being mocked, beaten, abandoned by friends and followers, tortured to death on a cross. There is almost nothing about the way we live our everyday lives, the choices we make, that enables us to see this as the action of God's power, working inexorably to set us free.

Easter day is perhaps a bit better: this is more how we might like God to behave. But even here we encounter disturbing truths, as the risen Jesus shows the marks of the nails in his hands and his feet, and refuses to confront those who were responsible for his death. Instead, he comes back from death to meet again with those few men and women who had been his faithless friends in life. So very few people meet the transcendent Lord, whom death itself cannot overcome. Then these very few are sent out to tell the whole world what God is like, and why God must be met, not in the trappings that human beings expect of him, but in the humility that he has chosen, in Jesus Christ.

The Christian witness insists that there is no way round this self-revelation of God. We cannot get to the majesty and saving power of God except in the way that God chooses to reveal it – in Jesus. There is, apparently, something compatible here, between the power of God and the humility of the human life and death of Jesus Christ. We do not instinctively understand this; it is so counter-intuitive, so alien to our definitions of achievement.

This, then, is the Lenten journey. During these weeks, we will try to slow ourselves down enough to pay attention to the ways of God. They are strange to us, and easy to miss. Along the way, our companions will be people who have walked this path before us, and can help us to understand that what we are encountering is the full might of God, which is God's humility. We are encountering the immensity of what God does to bring us home in Jesus Christ. God's humility is God's mercy. In this way – and no other – are we ransomed, healed, restored and forgiven. All other paths are of our own making and so cannot take us home to God, since only God knows the way to God.

In Lent, we are preparing to meet and to recognize the mercy of God. God's action is for us; we are the goal of what God is and does in Jesus Christ; it is all directed towards our salvation, which means our returning home, like the Prodigal Son, to find God waiting, with arms outstretched, to welcome us home to the feast that is laid for us (Luke 15:11–32). God acts on our behalf not because we are necessary to God, but because God is necessary to us. Like the Prodigal Son, we think we can make our own way in the world, but we simply cannot. We do not have the resources within ourselves to sustain us and give us everlasting joy. Only God has limitless resources of life, love, companionship and joy, and God is waiting to share them with us. They are not things that can be shared by force. Enforced life, love, companionship and joy become their opposites, instantly. So the Father waits, until the Prodigal returns.

Yet there is more. The infinite patience of God is more active than that of the father of the Prodigal, because God does more than wait; in Jesus Christ, God enters into the way of the Prodigal so that even here, while the Prodigal is still assuming that he is fine on his own, the love of the Father is present. The story of Jesus is significantly different from the parable of the Prodigal Son, because Jesus is God come to find us, not just waiting for us at the end, but present at every turn of the road. The parable of the Prodigal Son has one eye on those who objected that the father in the story was behaving improperly, and forgetting his dignity and authority. The older brother in the story is not sure that merciful humility is a good quality. He would prefer his father to make his profligate younger brother very, very sorry before forgiving him (Luke 15: 25–32).

Jesus tells this story, but the story he lives is a different one. The life of Jesus is the life of the God who leaves home to be with all of us Prodigals, in good times and in bad, and even into death. The life of Jesus means that we can turn and find God beside us, everywhere.

Lent helps us to refocus so that we may recognize the humble God, at our side. The patterns of God's ways are so strange, so intimate, that we can miss them altogether, and feel ourselves alone and abandoned, and having to find our own way home, if indeed there is any home to go to. Yet, all the time, it is a heartbeat away.

Lent also challenges us, as it challenges the brother of the Prodigal Son, to see that the good, the comfortable, the successful also need God's mercy, and can only find it in God's humility. The older brother, too, wants love and recognition, but he wants to believe that he has earned it himself, rather than receiving it as a gift. He needs to learn that love earned may always be forfeited again, whereas love that is based in the character of the one who loves can never be lost.

As we remember that we are dust, we come close to the fact that our lives will pass into nothingness unless they are held in the eternal meaning of God. God comes to find us, so that our dust may be filled with God's eternal life. God's humility is our salvation, because God deigns to care for us creatures of dust, and to invite them into the divine life. Walter Raleigh's poem acknowledges the pain of lives that seem to end in futility, but also the joy of knowing that God has resources beyond what we can imagine. Our Lent journey is to embrace our own powerlessness and insignificance with joy, as we learn to trust in the merciful humility of God, who comes to share our life so that it may be joined to God's.

EVEN such is Time, which takes in trust
Our youth, our joys, and all we have,
And pays us but with earth and dust;
Who in the dark and silent grave,
When we have wandered all our ways,
Shuts up the story of our days;
And from which earth, and grave, and dust,
The Lord shall raise me up, I trust.

PRACTICALITIES

Each chapter of the book that follows contains some biblical reflections on aspects of the life of Jesus, followed by an introduction to a Christian figure who helps to draw out the ongoing truth of the biblical insight. Each chapter also has some suggestions for response, starting with a focus on a biblical passage, and then setting some questions to help us make personal connections.

The hope is that this section at the end of each chapter may be used either for personal reflection, or to facilitate group discussion.

RIVER AND WILDERNESS

Lent is not primarily about 'giving things up', or denying ourselves. It is about finding ourselves. Along the way, it will often feel like a journey of self-abnegation, but that is because our 'selves' have so often been built on shaky foundations that will not bear the weight of the people God can see, looking through the eyes of Jesus. We may think we are what we have achieved, what we look like, what we own, what we do, but all of that can change, apparently putting us at risk, vulnerable to time and tide.

Jesus' time of discerning on what foundations his life will be built starts with an overwhelming affirmation, and that is where our Lent journey starts, too. Our Lent is usually counted as a period of 40 days, in which we try to attend to the decisions Jesus made, the temptations he faced, in his 40 days in the wilderness, before beginning his hectic public ministry. Yet the first thing we notice is that Jesus does not go out into the wilderness as a lonely hero, but in response to a gift. Jesus goes into the desert with the voice of the Father ringing in his ears, and with the force of the Holy Spirit with him. This is very much a journey from and into love.

The first reported action of the adult Jesus is to go and receive baptism from John the Baptizer (cf. Matthew 3: 12–17; Mark 1: 9–11; Luke 3: 21–22). John was enjoying a period of considerable popularity, and crowds came out to the River Jordan regularly, to be harangued for their sinfulness and then to receive a vigorous dunking as a symbol of their spiritual cleansing. Jesus goes, in all humility, to take part in this rite. He does not assume that, for him, there will be another, less degrading way of signalling his obedience to and dependence on God. He must have known, as all good Jews do, the story of Naaman and Elisha (cf. 2 Kings 5). Naaman was an army commander and a person of great importance, but all his might and wealth had not protected him from leprosy. He is persuaded, by a young Israelite slave girl, to go and consult with the prophet Elisha, and is desperate enough to take the advice. 2 Kings tells the story with masterly humour: Naaman arrives at the prophet's house, with a great retinue of chariots and horsemen, and with expensive gifts to buy healing. He is clearly expecting a transaction which will acknowledge his rank and importance, assuming that although he needs something from the prophet, it is his own initiative and resources that will get him what he wants.

The prophet does not even come out to meet him, but simply sends a message, telling Naaman to wash in the River Jordan. Naaman flies into a towering rage at this slight: 'Are not Abana and Pharpar, the rivers of Damascus, better than all the waters of Israel? Could I not wash in them and be clean?' (2 Kings 5: 12). Naaman's pride is hurt. He had expected impressive magic, as befitted his station, not this offhand, impersonal response. Perhaps he had even expected to be given something hard and dangerous to do, to win his reward. But when he is finally persuaded just to get into the river, and is healed, Naaman finally makes the right connection. This healing is nothing to do with his own status and achievements, and nor is it anything much to do with the magical powers of Elisha. 'Now I know,' says Naaman, 'that there is no God in all the earth except in Israel' (2 Kings 5: 15). Naaman, all that time ago, is making the connection that Lent encourages us to make: we are what we are because God is God.

Unlike Naaman, Jesus came to the Jordan without fanfare, and expecting no special treatment. He came with the crowds, to acknowledge the force and reality of sin, and his dependence on the action of God. The New Testament nowhere suggests that Jesus is protected from temptation to sin; indeed Hebrews 4: 15 specifically says otherwise: 'For we do not have a high priest who is unable to sympathize with our weaknesses, but we have one who in every respect has been tested as we are, yet without sin.' So there is no reason to believe that Jesus' request for baptism was anything other than a genuinely humble submission to God, as the only source of cleansing and healing. Jesus, the Son of God, does not play-act his identification with the human condition but is fully part of it. At the Jordan, he acknowledges the terrible power of sin, and on the Cross he will encounter it again, and in each case his only protection will be his humility, depending only on God to give judgement and meaning to life.

As Jesus comes out of the murky waters of the river, God the Spirit and God the Father tear apart the heavens to reach out to him in love. The Spirit rests on him as a dove, and the Father declares: 'You are my Son, the Beloved; with you I am well pleased' (Mark

1: 11). Matthew and Luke say, more temperately, that the 'heavens opened', rather than Mark's description of a violent rent that opens up a pathway between heaven, the proper dwelling place of God, and earth; but all agree, as does John (John 1: 32–34), about the presence of the Spirit, and the confirmation of Jesus as the Son of God. As yet, Jesus has done nothing but submit to baptism, and yet already he is beloved and gives pleasure to the Father. All he has 'achieved' is to acknowledge his dependence on God, which is more than many of us do in a lifetime, and is vital to everything that is to follow.

This is where Lent starts, with the voice of God, singing the praise of Jesus, the Son. Just as this affirmation calls Jesus into the wilderness, so it calls us, too. We are starting out from a place of loving acceptance, not from one of rejection; we are starting out with the certainty that God knows who we are and loves us, so that our explorations are to find out why that should be. We are exploring a reality that is given to us, not achieved by our own effort. Yet, glorious as this sounds, it is also terrifying, because if it starts with God and not with us, then we are not in control of it. Jesus steps into the River Jordan with such apparent ease, laying aside all claims to define himself, and that is our journey, too. So easy and so hard.

It is Mark, again, whose violent language highlights the fact that what is happening may be an insight into the humility of God, but that does not make it gentle. Mark says that the Spirit 'drove' Jesus into the wilderness (Mark 1: 12) immediately after the baptism. The gentle dove has turned into a fierce, driving wind. Matthew and Luke simply say that the Spirit 'led' Jesus there, but all are agreed that Jesus' first full, conscious demonstration of humble dependence on God called out the full force of evil to try to undermine it, snatch it away and close up that dangerous rent in the heavens, through which God speaks of love.

In Matthew and Luke's account of the temptation in the wilderness, it is clear that what the Evil One is trying to do is to undermine this baptismal revelation, that Jesus' power is that of dependence on the love of God; power comes from humility. The Devil tries to persuade Jesus that the love of God is a possession, to be used for his own ends, almost as though it is something he has achieved for himself. Cunningly, the Devil starts with the insidious 'if'. 'If you are the Son of God' (Luke 4: 3), 'then prove it to yourself and to others.' This method has proved very successful, over and over again, in luring people away from simple dependence on the nature of God. The Genesis creation account puts the same kind of question into the mouth of the cunning snake: 'What was it God said to you? Do you really believe that? Why not test it?' (Genesis 3: 1). Yet they had walked and talked with God, and should not have had any reason to doubt God, who had given them only good things, and shared creative power with them, wished them only joy.

Similarly, after the people of Israel have been rescued from Egypt by overwhelming power, led through the Red Sea as though along a garden path, miraculously fed and watered through the wilderness, Moses only has to be gone a few weeks, and they decide that God cannot be trusted and they will have to take matters into their own hands. They have seen such demonstrations of the love and vitality of God, and yet they want to make gods for themselves. 'Come, make gods for us, who shall go before us; as for this Moses, the man who brought us up out of the land of Egypt, we do not know what has become of him' (Exodus 32: 1). They convince themselves, against all the evidence, that Moses' God is only available through Moses, despite seeing Pharaoh and all his horsemen defeated, and the elements obeying God. They want convenient and amenable magic, to meet their needs; they are not interested in the nature and purpose of God.

Over and over again, the temptation to trust ourselves rather than depend on God has proved an effective one, and it is the one that the Devil uses on Jesus in the wilderness. 'Turn stones into bread,' suggests the Devil to the starving man. There is nothing inherently wrong with this suggestion; later on in his ministry, it will become clear that Jesus can miraculously feed others, as in the Feeding of the 5,000 (Matthew 14: 13–21), and they may be a bit hungry, but they are hardly starving. But Jesus responds: 'One does not live by bread alone'. It is no accident that what Jesus is quoting here is a reference to that journey of the people of Israel from slavery in Egypt to freedom in the Promised Land. Throughout that journey, God fed them, 'in order to make you understand that one does not live by bread alone, but by every word that comes from the mouth of the Lord' (Deuteronomy 8: 3). It is because Jesus willingly accepts this dependence that he is then able to feed the 5,000 and to continue to feed humanity with his own body and blood, daily. He is more interested in God than in what God can do for him.

The Devil moves on to more challenging temptations. He offers Jesus power, if Jesus will simply acknowledge that all power comes at a price, which is to acknowledge the rights of might. This is a fascinating one, which Luke has as the second temptation (Luke 4: 5–7) and Matthew as the final one (Matthew 4: 8–10). The Devil takes Jesus up to a vantage point from which he can see the world, in thrall, in slavery, because it belongs, so the Devil asserts, to him. All the kingdoms of the world, and so all the peoples of the world, presumably, are commodities, as far as the Devil is concerned; he will barter them, sublet them, trade with them, if that suits his purposes. If Jesus accepts this offer, he will step into a world where everything has a price, and we must be prepared to pay it to get what we want, and then we can do our best to get it back by extracting it from someone else.

But this is not the world that Jesus sees. With the Father's words still in his ears, he sees a world where love is freely given and received, because God's power is the power of merciful freedom from the Devil's economy, and a liberation into an economy of gift. It is Deuteronomy that Jesus quotes again, as he rejects this temptation: 'The Lord your God you shall fear; him you shall serve, and by his name alone you shall swear' (Deuteronomy 6: 13). Deuteronomy lays out the way of life that defines the people of God, giving them their character and their purpose in life, all of it flowing from their dependence on the gift of God and the action of God on their behalf. This is the world that Jesus sees, and from which he will live.

The Devil does not give up easily. He has not been used to losing in his relationships with human beings. The third temptation that is offered is again that Jesus should use his relationship with God for his own ends. It is another, understated, version of the 'if', attempting to get Jesus to doubt God and so to test what God's love actually means. Jesus is to place himself in danger, and require God to come rushing to his rescue, like superman to Lois Lane, because surely that is what love means? It must serve a purpose, rather than being valuable in its own right. It is Deuteronomy 6: 16, this time, that Jesus quotes: 'Do not put the Lord your God to the test', as though there is some method of weighing up different gods, and going for the one that is going to be most useful to us.

This is a hugely significant temptation, because if Jesus chooses to put himself and his needs, his safety, at the heart of what it is to be 'the beloved Son of God', then he chooses the usual human definition of God, powerful, invulnerable, demanding rather than giving. This kind of Son of God will not infuriate the imperial and religious powers, and will not end up on the Cross, so the story of Jesus ends here, in the wilderness, with the story of our salvation, which will only be won as the beloved Son goes to the hate-filled Cross. Jesus chooses the humble path of trusting in God, and allowing God to give him definition and purpose, rather than seizing them for himself.

It is striking that Jesus does 'choose'. The gospels describe a dialogue, with no apparent intervention by the Father and the Spirit, who have torn the heavens to make themselves accessible to the Son in human form. Yet in the wilderness they are silent, apparently absent, as Jesus chooses what it will mean for him to be the Beloved Son. Humbly, God stands aside and leaves everything in the hands of a lonely and famished man. In any journey of faith, there are these moments when it seems that we are alone with temptation, and that everything is weighted against God: other powers speak and act while God is dumb. But in this account, Jesus is aware that God is never dumb, even though the divine voice does not override the other voices around and demand precedence. Throughout these narratives, Jesus reaches for the guidance of God in scripture. The words are there, ready and waiting to be picked up, heard, put into action. The voice that speaks them in the wilderness is Jesus' voice, making the choice of dependence, the choice of belief in the reality and action of God, when there seems so little external evidence of the presence of God.

Jesus takes his own experience of God, and particularly those overwhelming words of love, 'You are my Beloved Son', and he weaves them into the great story of God's nature and action as told in scripture. He chooses that this will be who he is.

The profound meditations that we see in the gospel accounts of the temptation in the wilderness are about self-definition; in Jesus' case, he freely gives that task to the Father: only God will define Jesus, and under all circumstances, Jesus will be what God says he is: the Beloved Son, wanting and needing nothing else.

This is where Lent starts for us, too. We are already beloved by God, and God waits, humbly, while we try to work out if this is enough. It will mean putting aside other self-definitions, that may seem more obvious and dependable, but that will always take us back into the world where we are a commodity and treat others as such. If we are defined by what we do or have, then there will always be others who do and have more, and so threaten our self-definition. But if we are brave enough to let God tell us who we are, then we are always and for ever the beloved ones, alongside others equally beloved. Here is Lent.

It is part of the mad logic of the merciful humility of God that we know we are encountering God in Jesus Christ because Jesus is the human being who does not consider himself as God's equal. Philippians 2: 5–11 is a great early Christian hymn to this baffling reality: Christ humbles himself, and hands over power to others even to kill him, and that is what makes him worthy to be our Lord. It is tempting to imagine that for Jesus, unlike us, the dice are already loaded and the choices made easier because underneath, all the time, he always knows that he is God and can go back to that when his human career is over. But the truth is deeper than that: Jesus shows us something of the nature of the eternal God who is always like this, not just acting. It is only if God is always like this that we have hope that there is room for us in the eternal life of God.

AUGUSTINE AND THE HUMBLE GOD

This counter-intuitive discovery of the reality of God has to be made over and over again by human beings. Somehow, we keep reinventing a divine nature that is nothing like Jesus, but much more how we would 'do' God if we could. Over and over again, we are drawn back to God, sitting at our feet, while we drag the imaginary heavens looking for our image of God.

This analogy is one that Augustine of Hippo makes, in the fourth century, discovering the humble God who yet puts all other 'gods' to flight. He describes searching through the books of the Platonic philosophers, and discovering that, while there are some parallels between the way in which Christianity and Platonism describe the divine, what the Platonists do not have is the God who '"humbled himself being made obedient to death, even the death of the Cross"'.[1] And Augustine admits that, as a young man, 'To possess my God, the humble Jesus, I was not yet humble enough. I did not know what his weakness was meant to teach.'[2]

[1] *St Augustine: Confessions*, translated and edited by Henry Chadwick (OUP, 1991), p. 122.
[2] Ibid., p. 128.

This is how Augustine describes the logic of the merciful humility of God:

> In the inferior parts he built for himself a humble house of our clay. By this he detaches from themselves those who are willing to be made his subjects and carries them across to himself ... They are no longer to place confidence in themselves, but rather to become weak. They see at their feet divinity become weak ... In their weariness they fall prostrate before this divine weakness which rises and lifts them up.[3]

There are many different ways of describing the organizing principles of Augustine's spiritual search: a longing for sexual purity; a satisfactory response to the problem of sin and evil; a need to find an intellectually credible faith. But perhaps underpinning all of these is Augustine's encounter with the humility of God as the still centre of the spinning universe.

Augustine's *Confessions* is a spiritual and intellectual autobiography of a kind that was highly unusual in the fourth century. Some of its first readers were

[3]Ibid.

scandalized at Augustine's honesty, berating him for showing a Christian leader 'warts and all', rather than setting an edifying example for laypeople to follow. The whole book is an exercise in humility, as Augustine shows himself failing miserably to achieve fame or happiness until he throws himself down and allows God to lift him up.

The young Augustine was clearly a clever, attractive and arrogant young man. His early lack of respect for the Christian faith was motivated in part by the fact that his mother, Monica, was a Christian, and although Augustine clearly loved her, he also found her annoying, and did not consider her intellectually his equal, so had assumed that her faith was only for the ill-educated. Despising what was closest to home, Augustine embarked on a search for meaning, something to give coherence to his life and satisfy his intellectual and spiritual curiosity.

He left North Africa, without telling his mother, and got a prestigious job in the imperial court at Milan. Augustine does not labour the point, but he must have had extraordinary charm and intellectual ability to come from the obscure backwaters of the Roman Empire, and from a comparatively poor background, and yet find himself at the heart of power at such a young age.

In Milan, Augustine encountered the formidable Ambrose, bishop of Milan, whose political and intellectual status could not be questioned. Augustine was already seeing the flaws in the religious and philosophical system he had committed to, Manicheism. It had seemed to offer an intelligible account of the origins of the universe and the existence of evil, alongside a spirituality that suggested that it was possible for Augustine to live the kind of life he wanted to, and leave the essential 'divine' within himself unmarred. But both his head and his heart were growing sick of his way of life.

Monica pursued Augustine to Milan, and persuaded him, in the interests of his career, to give up his long-standing relationship with a young woman whom he had met in Carthage and brought to Italy with him, and with whom he had a much-loved son, Adeodatus. We know almost nothing about this young woman, except that she was the human love of Augustine's life, and some kind of an emotional anchor for him. When he sent her back to Africa, he never met her again, as far as we know, but nor did he then enter into the ambitious marriage that his mother had hoped for. Instead, he went off the rails completely, indulging in a series of empty liaisons.

At the same time, Augustine went regularly to hear Ambrose preach, and to sit in his presence, longing to question him, but particularly struck by the amount of time Ambrose spent in silence, reading and praying. Augustine saw so much in Ambrose that he admired and longed to imitate – his fame, his status in the world, his intelligence – but he knew that he was missing the essential Ambrose, the thing that made it possible for Ambrose to be celibate, and to be satisfied with a life given to the needs of others. 'I was attracted to the way, the Saviour himself,' Augustine writes, 'but was still reluctant to go along its narrow paths.'[4]

When things finally came to a head, Augustine was emotionally and physically worn out to the point of breakdown. He had come to hate his brilliant job, seeing it as a kind of slavery, no longer caring where it might take him; he found himself unable to give up sex, though despising himself for his weakness; he kept hearing stories of others who had managed to accept God and change their lives, and it tortured him that they were able to do what he was not. In one of the most moving 'conversion' stories in Christian

[4]Ibid., p. 133.

literature, Augustine describes sitting in turmoil, knowing that his current way of life was untenable: it was making him ill, because he could find no resting place for his heart and mind. As he sat, sobbing, in a friend's garden, he heard the voice of children, as though playing a game in another part of the garden. Their childish voices were crying: 'Pick up and read, pick up and read.' Looking around, Augustine saw an open copy of scripture, and he picked up and read part of St Paul's letter to the Romans, offering a freedom from conflicting desires, through encounter with the living God.[5]

It is surely no accident that this arrogant young man heard the voice of the humble God through childlike voices. Only the humble God could penetrate Augustine's armour. Like Naaman, Augustine received his healing through something simple and homely, not through his own valiant efforts.

The rest of Augustine's story flows from that moment. He gave up his job at the centre of the civilized world and went home to the backwater at the edge of the Roman Empire. On the way, Augustine describes a poignant moment of spiritual

[5]Ibid., pp. 152–3. Augustine read Romans 13: 13–14.

encounter, shared with his mother on her deathbed. After his conversion, Augustine was able to see his mother very differently, and hear the story of her own struggle with faith, including conquering an addiction to alcohol, and trying to live as a witness to Christ in a harsh marriage to an older and unfaithful man, Augustine's father. Through her patience and endurance, Monica succeeded in bringing Patricius to faith before he died. As she herself neared death, she and her son were discussing faith, and Augustine describes a moment when 'we extended our reach and in a flash of mental energy attained the eternal wisdom which abides beyond all things'.[6]

Although the vision could not last, it could be shared by an old, ill-educated woman and her brilliant son, both equally at home with 'eternal wisdom', in a way that Augustine would have found impossible to believe before he encountered the humble God.

Augustine spent the rest of his life as a Church leader and bishop in Hippo, North Africa. Although his writings became among the most influential in the whole of Christian history, claimed by Catholics and Reformers alike as the heart of their gospel, he

[6]Ibid., p. 172.

had little idea of this as he faithfully preached and pastored his people, living a life of celibacy and dedication that the young Augustine would have found intolerable.

Augustine's temptations were long-drawn-out, unlike Jesus' time of trial in the wilderness, but their character was not dissimilar. Jesus chose to be, always, in every situation, the Son of the Father, and to allow his life and death to be shaped only by this. Jesus chose to humble himself, and be only what God needed him to be. Augustine, too, handed over control of his destiny to God. He gave up his ambitions for fame, privilege and satisfaction through self-indulgence, and allowed himself to be directed by the humble God.

In Lent, Augustine's story is a helpful reminder that his conversion was also his salvation. Augustine's desire to run his own life was ruining his health and his happiness. Although he gave up many things to follow Jesus, he gained far more. Ironically, too, he got back so much of what he thought he had given up: Augustine of Hippo is famous, influential, beloved, where Augustine the ambitious Roman teacher of rhetoric would probably be unknown today. God was working in mercy as he humbled Augustine.

It is not only Augustine who encountered the merciful humility of God as the most powerful force imaginable. This was not just a tactic that God employed in Augustine's case, but an aspect of the character of God, working for our salvation, but in ways so gentle, so subtle, so apparently vulnerable, that it is easy to overlook the force of God's action, and its call to us to walk in the paths of humility, for our sake and for the sake of the world.

As we watch God at work, what begins to emerge is that God's merciful humility is the source of life. Jesus accepts his future as he rejects the Devil's temptations in the wilderness, and so he is the Son of God, who walks through death to make a pathway for us to come home to the Father.

SUGGESTED RESPONSES

- Start each morning of Lent by hearing God say to you: 'You are my beloved.'
- Read one of the accounts of the Temptation in the Wilderness, such as Matthew 4: 1–11:

> Then Jesus was led up by the Spirit into the wilderness to be tempted by the devil. He fasted forty days and forty nights, and afterwards he was famished. The tempter came and said to him, 'If you are the Son of God, command these stones to become loaves of bread.' But he answered, 'It is written,
>
> "One does not live by bread alone,
>
> but by every word that comes from the mouth of God."'
>
> Then the devil took him to the holy city and placed him on the pinnacle of the temple, saying to him, 'If you are the Son of God, throw yourself down; for it is written,
>
> "He will command his angels concerning you,"
>
> and "On their hands they will bear you up,
>
> so that you will not dash your foot against a stone."'

Jesus said to him, 'Again it is written, "Do not put the Lord your God to the test."'

Again, the devil took him to a very high mountain and showed him all the kingdoms of the world and their splendour; and he said to him, 'All these I will give you, if you will fall down and worship me.' Jesus said to him, 'Away with you, Satan! for it is written,

"Worship the Lord your God,

and serve only him."'

Then the devil left him, and suddenly angels came and waited on him.

- The temptations seem to be for Jesus to take care of his own immediate needs, to ensure his own personal safety, and to win fame and power. What would be your greatest temptation?
- Jesus chooses obedience to God as the principle that will govern his life. Do you have a principle that governs your life, on the basis of which you make your important decisions? If so, are you content with it? If not, what might you like it to be?

- Jesus turns to scripture to help him when God seems far away. What do you turn to in times of fear and uncertainty?

FURTHER READING ON AUGUSTINE

Augustine, *Confessions*, edited and translated by Henry Chadwick, OUP, 2008.

Peter Brown, *Augustine of Hippo: A Biography*, University of California Press, 2013.

Suzanne M. Wolfe, *The Confessions of X*, Thomas Nelson, 2016. (This is a novel about the relationship between Augustine and the unnamed mother of his son.)

2

HUMBLE BEGINNINGS

It is ironic that we do not know exactly when Jesus was born. The Western world has, for 2,000 years, counted dates from the 'year of our Lord', but with a system devised by human beings, not dictated by God. In the seventeenth century, Archbishop Ussher famously believed that he was able to date the creation of the world to 4004 BC, and he is just one of many examples of the persistent desire to get straight what God has apparently left in a bit of a mess.

God just did not bring the right people to witness the birth of Jesus Christ, the Son of God; there was, apparently, no one there who was capable of writing down the time and date. Decades later, Luke does his best: he tells us that he 'investigated carefully ... To write an orderly account' (Luke 1: 3). Painstakingly, he finds such external markers as he can: the Emperor Augustus, who reigned from 27 BC to AD 14, and Quirinius, governor of Syria, who lived from circa 40 BC to AD 21, are identified as in power at the time of Jesus' birth. But there is considerable uncertainty about whether the census Luke describes actually took place, and even if it did, as a low-key, bean-counting exercise on the part of a local district jobsworth, it does not help to fix the date very precisely.

Luke is aware, even as he sets out to collect all the facts that he can, that he is probably working against the subversive humility of God. Theophilus, for whom Luke writes, wants to 'know the truth', by which, presumably, he means indisputable facts, and Luke provides what he can; but he also witnesses God's strange lack of interest in ensuring that there is proof of his doings; Luke is a good enough historian to tell what he found, and not to add in things that would have made his story more palatable for 'Theophilus'.

Luke starts his 'orderly account' with a good priestly family, Zechariah and Elizabeth, both of impeccable lineage, just the kind of people God should be putting at the heart of his action. But all too quickly, Zechariah the priest is doubting the word of an angel, and he is struck dumb, while his wife Elizabeth, pregnant when she had given up all hope, stays confined in her own home for five months (Luke 1: 24), waiting.

Elizabeth knows that the real story has not yet begun; she knows that she is a supporting actor, despite her miraculous pregnancy. Elizabeth's son, John the Baptist, learns from the womb onwards this peaceful attention to the thread of God's story. When, in later life, John and Jesus meet as adults, John says: 'He must increase, but I must decrease' (John 3: 30). John is not the Messiah, just as Elizabeth is not the mother of God.

Quietly, in her own home, Elizabeth waits, savouring God's attention, even though she is not the heart of the action, nurturing the child, even though he is not the Messiah. She waits for the prelude to be over and for the main action to start. 'In the sixth month the angel Gabriel was sent by God' (Luke 1: 26) to a girl called Mary, and the curtain goes up. The conversation between Gabriel and Mary is so different from the one five months earlier, between Gabriel and Zechariah. Zechariah is in the sanctuary of the Temple, performing his priestly function of offering incense, while all the people wait outside, praying. The setting is perfect, hushed, holy, surrounded by prayer and the sweet smell of incense. If ever a stage was set for an angelic appearance, surely this was it. Yet Zechariah, for whom angels should have been a specialist topic, was terrified; and as soon as he recovered from his fear, he was rudely incredulous.

The encounter between Mary and the angel went very differently. There is no stage set – Luke does not even tell us where it happened; there is no lead-up, telling us of all Mary's qualifications for this conversation; yet Mary is 'perplexed' where Zechariah was 'terrified'. Crucially, Zechariah asks for proof: 'How will I know that this is so?' (Luke 1: 18), and he is, not surprisingly, slapped down by the angel. 'I am Gabriel', what more proof do you want, the angel says. Mary, on the other hand, points out the obstacles to the angel's plan – she is a virgin – but she asks nothing else, nothing to take back to her hurt fiancé as evidence of her good faith, nothing to show to the gossiping neighbours, as proof of her purity, nothing to reassure herself, through the years to come, that she had not deceived herself about the conversation. Mary simply says: 'Here I am, the servant of the Lord', 'yes, I will do this'.

Later generations of Christians went on to justify God's choice of Mary by investing her with a miraculous childhood and holy parents, making her worthy in ways that we can understand. But that seems to undermine the point that Luke helps us to see: Zechariah was 'worthy', in all outward forms, but he muffed it. Mary is simply willing. The Magnificat is Mary's theology: what God sees in her is precisely her 'lowliness', which gives her insight into the character of God, whose mercy 'scatters the proud', 'brings down the powerful', so that the hungry can be filled. God's mercy makes space for those who are thought to be of no account, and Mary knows herself to be one of them.

This is what Elizabeth has been patiently waiting for, this great hymn to the mysterious mercy of God. Elizabeth, the descendant of priests, the wife of a priest, the woman blessed with a child in old age, curtsies to Mary, the girl from nowhere, pregnant and unmarried. She recognizes what God saw in Mary, 'blessed is she who believed that there would be a fulfilment of what was spoken to her by the Lord' (Luke 1: 45). Where Zechariah demanded proof, Mary trusted. Luke tells us that Mary and Elizabeth spent three months together, and although we are given no details of their conversations, we can imagine the comfort, the strength that they drew from one another. Whose choice was it that Mary did not stay for the birth of John? Elizabeth's, I think. Elizabeth would not want the young woman to see the horror of childbirth, and to live in fear of the time when her own child was to be born. Elizabeth sends Mary home, rejoicing. And it seems that Zechariah, too, spent those months well, for when his child is finally born, Zechariah is humbled. He does not attempt to give the boy a family name, asserting his ancestry, his rights, his credentials; instead, he follows his wife's lead, and names him John. Zechariah has learned something of the new order.

Luke's 'orderly account' comes back again and again to the way in which God's action relativizes the normal standards of a story about the birth of someone important. After putting Zechariah soundly in his place, the Roman Empire comes on next, playing a bit part. Augustus, one of the most successful and feted of Roman emperors, is used simply to engineer what is almost a private divine joke. Micah 5: 2 says that 'one who is to rule in Israel, whose origin is from of old' will come from Bethlehem. The census, which is supposed to remind the subject nation that they are just so many counters, to be pushed around to suit Roman convenience, turns out to be the means of bringing Mary and Joseph to Bethlehem, for the birth of the child. No wonder Mary and Joseph make the journey, despite Mary's advanced pregnancy, and the crowded town and inhospitable conditions: they can see and share God's joke; of course, the emperor, whether he knows it or not, is working under God's command. Of course, the baby will be born in Bethlehem, as the prophet from centuries ago predicted.

Perhaps for Joseph this private confirmation that God is in charge, even of empires, may have offered some consolation. Joseph is a fitting collaborator with God's strange ways of working. If Luke tells us the story from Mary's point of view, Matthew tells us Joseph's part. Mary says yes to the angel with no apparent thought for her poor bewildered fiancé. It may be that her trust in Joseph is so deep that she knows she can rely upon him, but there is no mention at all of him and his role in the angelic exchange, no suggestion that he is blessed among men, as she is to be among women. Mary steps out into dangerous isolation when she accepts her role as the mother of the Son of God, and she does so without preconditions. She does not demand that the angel should guarantee her safety – she takes that for granted.

And so Joseph, too, is called to step out of the usual patterns of decent behaviour and become Mary's shield. Matthew tells us that this was not Joseph's original plan: when he learns about the pregnancy, he intends to act decently towards Mary, not shaming her publicly, not showing her and others the anger and hurt he must have felt, but nonetheless distancing himself and ending the relationship (Matthew 1: 19). But when the angel comes to Joseph in a dream he, like Mary, says yes: 'When Joseph awoke from sleep, he did as the angel of God commanded him' (Matthew 1: 24).

There is a poignancy to Joseph, recruited to stand at the edge, vital but ignored. Joseph does not sing of God's favour, or the strength of God's subversive power; yet he lives out of that understanding of God, just as Mary does. He believes his dream, unlikely as it is, calling him to trust that this is indeed the way in which God is coming to save his people. It must have comforted Joseph's heart when the summons came to travel to Bethlehem, with a heavily pregnant wife, so that the child could be born into the fulfilment of prophecy. Joseph had been acting on the strength of a dream, which no one else could confirm, but now, a Roman governor decrees a great movement of peoples, so that Jesus will be born in Bethlehem of Judea.

In the years ahead, Joseph humbly carries out his duties. Guided again by an angelic dream, he takes his family to Egypt to avoid Herod's threat, presumably disrupting his business, leaving his home, just for the sake of this child who is not his (Matthew 2: 13–15). Even in this, he is acting almost as a puppet, fulfilling an old prophecy: 'Out of Egypt I have called my son' (Matthew 2: 15). Joseph does all the necessary things for the child, naming and circumcising, finding the money for the right offerings, bringing the child into the family of God's people and teaching him the law, giving him all the earthly benefits that are at Joseph's disposal. In later life, Jesus is called 'the carpenter's son from Nazareth' (Matthew 13: 55), even though the carpenter himself has no more scenes to play. Joseph simply fades away, his work done. Mary is there in the Upper Room at Pentecost, but there is no word of Joseph. That may seem unfair obscurity, for one who has played such a significant part, but the narrative we are tracing warns us against being dazzled by those who think they are the star of the show. Joseph responds to God, does what he is asked, and then steps back again. God trusted Joseph with something of vital importance, and Joseph did not let God down. In God's eyes, Joseph is a hero, and one after God's own heart – a humble and merciful hero, requiring no applause.

Joseph does not have to undergo the bitter and painful journey that we walk with Mary. Mary does not at first understand, as Joseph instinctively does, that her role is limited. It seems that Mary thought she was going to be alongside Jesus, part of his ministry, all through. Mary's ideal picture is the one we see at the Wedding at Cana, where Jesus is very much the local boy, known as Mary's son (John 2: 1–11). Mary prompts him, as though by right, to perform the miraculous transformation of water into wine, and Jesus does it. But the enigmatic little exchange between Mary and Jesus is the first hint of troubles to come. Jesus says to Mary, quite sternly: 'Woman, what concern is that to you and to me? My hour has not yet come' (John 2: 4). It is the first warning to Mary that she will not be able to dictate the course of Jesus' life.

Later, we see Mary and her other children trying to get Jesus back under control, trying to remind him of his first loyalty to them, to reshape Jesus' ministry in ways more acceptable to them. It is painful to hear the rebuff: 'Who is my mother, and who are my brothers?' (Matthew 12: 48). It is as though Mary has forgotten her own theology, poured out in the Magnificat. There, she rejoiced that God overturns the natural order, but now she longs for a natural order again, where sons obey their mothers and put them first. We know that Mary relearns the truth of God, standing at her son's Cross, then seeing the empty tomb and receiving the outpouring of the Spirit. But her journey is a salutary lesson to us all, that if we worship the God who puts down the mighty from their thrones to make space for the humble and weak, he will do the same to us, if we become the mighty and refuse to see the humble.

In the gospels, we go very swiftly from Jesus' birth to his adulthood. But Jesus' choices in the wilderness have their roots in earlier choices, made by others who also understand the call to humility. We have no excuse for forgetting those whom God calls to witness to the changing order. As Jesus steps out into public ministry, we remember the shepherds, out in the fields, visited by the hosts of heaven and personally invited to the cradle of the Son of God. Shepherds spend most of the time out in the fields, guarding and pasturing the flocks, so they are hardly the best people to broadcast news in the towns and villages. They go back to their flocks rejoicing at what they have seen, and that is apparently enough for God. God has always had a soft spot for shepherds, from David onwards, and the child whom the shepherds came to worship grew up to describe himself, quite often, as one of them, preferring that description to 'king' or 'messiah'. There is something about shepherding that lies close to the heart of how God works; shepherds feed and care for sheep, who can give them little in the way of understanding or affection in return; shepherds protect the weak sheep against the strong predators all around; shepherds risk their own comfort and safety for the sheep. No wonder God invites them to Bethlehem.

After the shepherds come the wise men. They are strangers, not part of the family of God's people Israel. They have no interest in the Messiah, the saviour of Israel. Yet their skills of stargazing and divination win them, too, an invitation to meet the new king. We are not told where they come from or how far they travelled, or even how many of them there are; they are described as 'wise men from the East' (Matthew 2: 1). They bring exotic and valuable gifts, so perhaps they were expecting to win favour and to be offered prestigious places at the court of the new king who is powerful enough to have his own star. Yet they are utterly satisfied with their meeting, 'overwhelmed with joy' (Matthew 2: 10), even though it cannot have been what they hoped for when they set out. They, like the shepherds, worship and go home rejoicing. Their story, too, signals God's ways. There is space for them at the cradle, simply because they came. They are not the right race or religion, they do not consult the scriptures or know the prophecies, but they see the star and they follow it to their heart's desire.

As we read the gospels and move from these strange and unstrategic beginnings to the moment when the adult Jesus begins his ministry, it should come as no surprise that the base of his operations is not among the powerful and influential but with fishermen, peasants and sinners. But it is easy to forget that 30 years have passed. The gospel writers pass over this time almost completely. Luke gives us one glimpse of the boy Jesus, confounding the experts in the Temple (Luke 2: 46–47). What the experts had learned laboriously over the years seemed instinctive to Jesus, even as a boy. Luke shows us the family of Jesus as devout and properly observant Jews, having their son circumcised, taking him to the Temple for the great festivals when he is old enough, and so, presumably, Jesus, like other little Jewish boys, would have learned the Torah and how to live by it. But in this vignette of the child in the Temple, Luke shows us something more than the usual engagement with scripture: it is as though we are seeing the relationship between the written word and the Word incarnate, here in this interaction: 'all who heard him were amazed at his understanding' (Luke 2: 47).

If the gospels were novels, we would expect so much more about Jesus' childhood, about his relationships with parents and friends, about how his miraculous power and authority were visible, even in the young boy. Instead, we have almost nothing for this, the longest period of Jesus' life. The gospels concentrate on the two or three short years of Jesus' public ministry, ending in his bitter death and mysterious resurrection, and tell us nothing of the approximately 30 years that go before. It seems profligate of God not to use these years, but to leave them hidden – 30 years of God the Son, living an ordinary human life, wasted. Unless, of course, they are not wasted, but fruitful in ways that are not immediately obvious to us. The man Jesus does not come out of nowhere. Like us, he grows, develops, learns; like us, he becomes who he is; he is not born full-grown, but grows into the one we meet in the gospels. The day-to-day encounters, choices, joys and sorrows of growing up help to make him who he is, and so are part of God's self-gift to us in Jesus. It is not wasteful simply to be; Jesus waits patiently, living his life quietly, unremarked by a wider audience, until the time is right, and then he is ready; everything is there, the fruits of those hidden years, grown to fullness.

These Nazareth years are part of God's humble gift. They give a kind of nobility and purposefulness to what can seem to us like emptiness. The leisureliness of God's action in Jesus through all those years gives a weight to our own mundane existence, filling it with potential. If Jesus was willing to take years, increasing 'in wisdom ... and in divine and human favour' (Luke 2: 52), then that gives purpose to our own years of growing, learning, making daily, unexciting choices that are yet the material that forms us. This is purposeful living, those hidden years suggest; it is enough simply to relate to God and to each other, and let God do with that what is necessary. Our Lent may start with the confrontation in the wilderness, and the sharp sting of temptation, but it has to continue in daily choices, for 40 days and then for life.

JULIAN OF NORWICH

We may long for our lives to be exciting and notable, to impact others and bring us fame and approval, but

God often seems to judge differently. Those secret Nazareth years are a hint, a clue, to the quiet, almost subterranean action of God, who is never wasteful, but also who is not dazzled by the obvious, as we are. The humble God asks us to trust that humility is fruitful, even if it is hidden. Milton, struggling with blindness that seemed, in his day, to put an end to his usefulness, learned the lesson: 'They also serve who only stand and wait.' Waiting, in God's company, is worthwhile, as the child, growing into the man, Jesus of Nazareth, demonstrates.

One of the most striking examples of God's economy is the story of Julian of Norwich. Julian's book *Revelations of Divine Love* is now a beloved classic of the Christian life, but for centuries it was virtually unknown, and Julian herself can have had no knowledge or expectation of her future impact.

We know very little about Julian – even her name probably comes from the church of St Julian in Norwich, where she lived for many years as an anchorite, in a tiny room attached to the church, which she left only in death. We glean little hints about her life from her writing, and from one or two glimpses of her in others; for example, we know that she was visited by Margery Kempe, a

Christian mystic, who writes of a visit to Julian, probably in the early decades of the fifteenth century. We do not know exactly when Julian was born or when she died. We do not know if she had been married or had children, though if she had, they appear to be dead by the time she writes. Julian does not expect her readers to be interested in her biography or personality; the only thing she thinks worth describing in detail is what God shows her. She records that when she was about 30 she had an illness that brought her close to death. The priest who came to administer the last rites held a crucifix before her face and she found herself in the presence of the dying Jesus, watching his suffering, and the great drops of blood falling down his agonized face. While this might have been a terrifying vision for one facing death herself, in fact what Julian felt was the depth of the love of God, who is willing to go to any lengths to be with us, even in suffering.

Over the next few hours and days, Julian received a series of 16 'showings', or revelations, all centring on the unshakeable love of God. When she recovered, she wrote down what she had seen and heard and then, over the next 20 or 30 years, she retreated to her 'cell', a tiny room, walled into the side of St

Julian's church, where she could observe the services going on, and where people could come and visit her, speaking to her through a window, but from where she herself never ventured out again. Instead, she continued to reflect on the visions, and to distil their theological meaning, their insight into the nature of God. These works, her initial account and then the longer reflection, usually called the Short Text and the Long Text, are, as far as we can tell, the earliest book to be written in English by a woman. But although they were preserved, they were not widely circulated or read, unlike, for example, the works of Julian's contemporary, Walter Hilton, whose *Scale of Perfection* survives in numerous manuscripts and was widely read not just in England but across the continent. Yet, although Hilton is still read nowadays, it is Julian, with her homely and intensely intimate visions, who has captured the modern imagination. It is as though God stored up the work, ready for the right time. There are hardly any near-contemporary manuscripts of Julian's work, and it came close to being lost entirely. Its survival seems almost miraculous.

Julian's theology is daring and controversial, though written in a gentle, unprovocative style, as an account of her own personal experience, rather than as a theological treatise. Julian claims to have been 'a simple and uneducated creature',[1] which almost certainly meant that she had received no formal theological education, and did not know Latin well enough to write in what was the universal language of the educated in medieval Europe. Yet Julian's reflections lead her to conclusions that were directly contrary to some of the accepted theological ideas of her day. From the moment she sees the bleeding, dying face of Christ, reaching out in love to her on her deathbed, Julian is convinced that the most important thing we need to know about God is that God loves us. Julian sees nothing wrathful or judging in the character of God, but only nurturing love. She writes, simply: 'it is absolutely impossible that God should be angry.'[2] The medieval depictions of the torments of hell awaiting those who fail to satisfy God seem like another universe to the one that Julian inhabits. Julian speaks of God's love as 'motherly', in a way that is more than simply metaphorical. This is the reality of the character of Jesus. Julian describes how human mothers give birth to children who must die, but

[1] *Revelations of Divine Love,* edited and translated by Clifton Wolters (Penguin Books, 1966), p. 63.
[2] Ibid., p. 137.

'Jesus, our true Mother ... bears us to joy and eternal life'.[3] Human mothers suckle their children, 'but our beloved Mother, Jesus, feeds us with himself'.[4] Julian seems to be referring to the mythological image of the mother pelican, tearing its breast to feed its young, as a symbol of Jesus, who tears his own body on the Cross, and offers it to us as food and drink, the stuff of life, in the Eucharist.

In another of her 'showings', Julian sees a tiny hazelnut, and is told in the vision that it represents everything that exists. It is insignificant, fragile, with no power to protect itself or prolong its own existence, so how can it continue? Julian asks. As she gazes at the hazelnut world, this is what she realizes: 'The first is that God made it, the second is that God loves it, the third is that God sustains it.'[5] Nothing is required of the hazelnut, because all is supplied by God.

Julian is so persuaded of the overwhelming power of God's love that she cannot ascribe any ultimate power to evil or to human sin. She says that when she tried to understand how sin came into being at all, God simply told her: 'Sin was necessary.' God

[3]Ibid., p. 169.
[4]Ibid., p. 170.
[5]Ibid., p. 68.

gives no further explanation, but follows this strange statement with a much fuller positive one: 'but all is going to be all right; it is all going to be all right; everything is going to be all right.'[6] We cannot understand sin, and should not over-fixate on it, for it is as nothing in the face of the love of God, which will always have the last word. Julian's conviction is that this is not a statement of blind optimism but of absolute faith in the nature of God.

When Julian asks, towards the end of her book, for a summary of what she has learned, the Lord answers: 'You would know our Lord's meaning in this thing? Know it well. Love was his meaning. Who showed it to you? Love. What did he show you? Love. Why did he show it? For love. Hold on to this and you will know and understand love more and more. But you will not know or learn anything else – ever!'[7]

Julian's book is rightly called *Revelations of Divine Love*, and her years of meditations on her original 'showings' simply deepened her certainty that, from the moment her dying eyes saw the gouts of blood dripping from the crucified Christ, what she

[6]Ibid., p. 103.
[7]Ibid., p. 212.

was seeing was the loving heart of her creator and redeemer.

In a medieval town in England, Jesus comes to meet a woman of no particular education or influence and reveals his heart to her. Her response is to wall herself up in a tiny room attached to a church and never to leave it again. She does write down an account of what she has seen, and it is enough to feed her prayer and imagination for the rest of her life. But she makes no great effort to disseminate her manuscript or to preach what she has discovered, far and wide. Quietly, Julian sits in her cell, offering hope and comfort to those who were able to make their way to her window, but seeing those few, presumably, and her own personal devotion, as her life's work. For centuries after her death, few people read the *Revelations*, few seemed struck by its bold theology; one or two copies of the manuscript lay peacefully in one or two libraries until, in the nineteenth century, translators discovered it again and began to make it more widely available.

The riches of Julian's theology have proved to be the treasure trove that our age longs for. Her unselfconscious use of feminine, maternal imagery about God comes to us as a promise of the inclusiveness of God's nature; her message of the steadfast, unalterable, unjudging love of God reaches out to those who have felt excluded by organized religion; her profound hopefulness reaches out to a world in turmoil, offering us the dream of the merciful tide of God's power that cannot be diverted by human failure.

God's activity may sometimes look wasteful, inefficient or even lacking in potency. But the Nazareth years, and stories like that of Julian of Norwich, suggest otherwise. God's timescale may not be ours, but that means that we have something to learn, rather than that God should change. When Jesus begins his public ministry, he is equipped with all the gifts he needs, garnered through the years of growing, learning, becoming, privately, out of our sight. When Julian's great theology is rediscovered, it comes to a world hungry for precisely this assurance. God's action is sometimes spacious, slow and hard to comprehend in its apparent lack of force, but it seems that God is to be trusted. God may work quietly, humbly, apparently at the mercy of greater forces and even accidents of history, but this is still God at work, and love is still God's meaning.

SUGGESTED RESPONSES

- Start each morning of Lent by hearing God say to you: 'You are my beloved.'
- Luke 2: 52: 'And Jesus increased in wisdom and in years, and in divine and human favour.' Are there periods of your life that could be summed up in a sentence? Looking back, can you see how this apparently fallow time helped to form you?
- Are there periods of your life that you look back on with regret? Can you see that they, too, may have given you important insights and resources?
- Who do you think have been the most important influences in your life, and why?
- Are there things in your life that you feel have been wasted?

FURTHER READING ON JULIAN OF NORWICH

Revelations of Divine Love, translated and edited by Clifton Wolters, Penguin Classics, 1966.

Enfolded in Love: Daily Readings with Julian of Norwich, edited by Robert Llewellyn, DLT, 2004.

Denys Turner, *Julian of Norwich: Theologian*, Yale University Press, 2013.

Margaret Coles, *The Greening*, Hay House, 2013. (This is a novel about a modern encounter with Julian's writing.)

3

HOW TO WIN FRIENDS AND INFLUENCE NOBODY

In Lent, as we walk alongside Jesus, trying to understand more of the merciful humility of God, the company he keeps gives us further clues. Almost the first thing Jesus does at the start of his ministry is to gather around himself a disparate group of friends, and to start to offend the people who might have been able to promote his agenda. He seemed to have a clear strategy, but one that is baffling by most ordinary standards. His ministry was certainly not designed either to win influential friends or to avoid conflict. In Jesus' life, 'humility' is a dynamic and forceful quality, with no suggestion of passivity or weakness. God's merciful humility is powerful, an expression of the vitality and freedom of God. God is not forced to be humble because he has no power to be anything else, but because this humility changes the balance of power altogether, as we see in the life, ministry, death and resurrection of Jesus.

Mark's gospel describes the calling of the first disciples with the brevity that is characteristic of this gospel writer. The style of Mark's gospel emphasizes the speed and urgency of Jesus' mission. Within the first few paragraphs, Jesus has been baptized and has faced the temptation in the wilderness; John the Baptist has been arrested, and at once, 'Jesus came to Galilee, proclaiming the good news of God' (Mark 1: 14). The 'good news', the 'gospel' that Jesus announces, is that now is the decisive time. 'The Kingdom of God has come near.' God is too close for comfort, now, and decisions about the direction of our lives cannot be put off any longer. As people encounter Jesus, they face the critical decision – for him, or against him, and that is a decision either for or against God.

It seems unfair that this should be so. There is nothing obvious about Jesus that alerts people to the fact that they are making the most important decision of their lives as they approach him. Hebrews 12: 18 describes what we would expect in an encounter with God: 'a blazing fire, and darkness, and gloom, and a tempest, and the sound of a trumpet, and a voice whose words made the hearers beg that not another word be spoken to them.' Instead, here is a young man, of no obvious importance, no wealth, no powerful family background, and people are expected to be attentive enough to see that the encounter with him is the pivotal moment in their lives.

As the gospel story unfolds, it is clear that there is an indefinable something about Jesus, often described as 'authority' (cf. Mark 1: 27). Few people who meet Jesus are indifferent to him, but it gradually emerges that the more institutional authority people have, whether imperial or religious, the less they like Jesus. There is something uncomfortably challenging about him, as though he does not accept the obvious badges of power, and seems to feel that he can judge them by some higher standard. Jesus' failure to acknowledge and respect those who hold power condemns his mission to inevitable failure, the failure that culminates in the Cross. He seems to show an almost deliberate misunderstanding of how the world works.

That contrariness starts with the people Jesus calls to be his closest friends and allies in his campaign. In Mark's gospel, Jesus' mission starts with a walk along the shore of the Sea of Galilee, gathering up the men who will be the heart of his team, but who will also misunderstand him and ultimately desert him. Yet they have the great merit of seeing and responding to Jesus' 'authority'. Jesus calls Simon Peter, Andrew, James and John to leave everything and follow him, and they do (Mark 1: 16–20). They are fishermen, involved in the family business, but at one word from Jesus they leave their nets and their boats and go with him. Perhaps they thought they were just taking an afternoon off to hear what this new teacher had to say, but in fact they were making a momentous decision, that changed the whole course of their lives.

The disciples are comfortingly and challengingly familiar. They react as Jesus' followers have done ever since. All through Jesus' busy, demanding ministry, these disciples share in times of wild exhilaration, when Jesus performs miracles and the crowds flock round with adulation; they bask in his reflected glory, when the crowds come and beg them for access to Jesus; they grow their own skills and understanding in exercising ministry. But they also misunderstand Jesus consistently, particularly in relation to his goal. They see his power and the influence that he could wield, and they assume that he must want to do what they themselves would do if they could. The moment that most sums this up is when James and John come and ask Jesus: 'Grant us to sit, one at your right hand and one at your left, in your glory' (Mark 10: 36). James and John have assumed that Jesus' mission is to seize power, and they are negotiating for seats in the Cabinet of the new government. Gently, patiently, Jesus tries to explain to them that his 'glory' will be to drink the bitter cup of suffering. But however many times he tried to explain this, the disciples did not understand. Their terrified flight when Jesus was arrested demonstrated that this was the last thing they expected. They saw it as defeat, not the goal towards which Jesus' whole life had been directed.

It is easy to mock the disciples, and to wonder how they could have been so stupid, but the history of the Christian Church bears witness to the fact that few of Jesus' disciples throughout the centuries have been willing to follow the pattern of Jesus' authority, and rely on the power of God's humility to change the world.

Yet that inner circle of disciples felt and responded to Jesus' authority. They left their homes and families, their settled ways of life, to follow him on the roads; they stayed with him until, humanly speaking, it looked as though everything was over. They simply did not have the interpretive framework to understand

Jesus' mission, because it was so counter-intuitive. After Jesus' death and resurrection, another of Jesus' followers wrote, bluntly, that Christians should realize that if God calls people like us into fellowship, then God cannot be operating with normal rules. In 1 Corinthians, Paul writes: 'Consider your own call, brothers and sisters: not many of you were wise by human standards, not many were powerful, not many were of noble birth. But God chose what is foolish in the world to shame the wise; God chose what is weak in the world to shame the strong; God chose what is low and despised in the world, things that are not, to reduce to nothing things that are' (1 Corinthians 1: 26–28). The Corinthians can hardly have been flattered to hear such things about themselves, but the point is central to Paul's theology of the 'foolishness of God'. God's people are not strategically recruited for their leadership qualities, their gifts and their talents; they do not contribute something vital to God's plans, which would otherwise be incomplete; they are invited to rely on the love of God, which has room for any who will respond.

Even if the disciples were not able to reflect on the unlikeliness of their own calling, and continued to think that Jesus had seen their great qualities and chosen them accordingly, they must have had some hesitations about the nature of his campaign, and the company they found themselves keeping. The inner circle of disciples seems to have been a strange cross-section of the population. Mark 3: 13–19 gives a list of the Twelve, who were to be the foundation of the New Israel, representing the twelve tribes of God's people, drawn from different political and social backgrounds, with nothing in common but Jesus. Furthermore, Luke 8 explicitly states what is implicit in all the gospel accounts, which is that women, too, were part of Jesus' inner circle. Luke 8: 2 speaks, at first, of 'some women', who are named, and then 'many others', so the impression is that, as with the male disciples, there was an inner circle of dedicated, identifiable women, and an outer circle. These disciples, too, are travelling with Jesus 'through cities and villages, proclaiming and bringing the good news of the kingdom of God' (Luke 8: 1).

As Jesus travels about, teaching and healing, most of the people who respond to him are outsiders, or those on the margins of society. He heals beggars, lepers, women; he feeds the hordes who have followed him and do not have the wherewithal to feed themselves; he talks to and receives ministry from women. His disciples are shocked when they find him talking to a Samaritan woman at a well (John 4: 1–43). The shock waves radiate out from several different centres – she is an unaccompanied woman and a Samaritan heretic, and no better than she should be. Yet Jesus has a deep and self-revelatory conversation with her, tackling not just her life and needs but profound theological themes, about the schism between Jews and Samaritans, about the nature of God, who seeks out 'true worshippers' (John 4: 23) across such barriers, and about the water of life. He does not patronize her either by turning a blind eye to her chaotic family life or by assuming she is too stupid to understand him. As a result of Jesus' trust in this unlikely woman, her whole village is converted. Yet we do not know her name.

The confusion about another significant incident involving a woman and Jesus is ironically appropriate, and, again, leaves us with uncertainty about her name. All four gospels tell of a woman who anoints Jesus with a costly oil, in a way that all the onlookers feel to be inappropriate in the extreme. Matthew 26: 6–16, Mark 14: 3–11 and John 12: 1–8 all set this incident in Bethany, and John names the woman as Mary, the sister of Lazarus, though the other two do not. They all agree that it happens at a time of escalating tension between Jesus and the religious authorities, and that Judas is so revulsed by the whole situation that it precipitates him into his act of betrayal.

The woman's action at this pivotal moment is a point of stillness and recognition. Jesus sees that this woman, alone of all his disciples, has understood that he is not going to avoid the fate that awaits him, he is not going to use his power to escape or to start a revolution; he is going to die. It is as though the woman's prophetic gift has enabled her to see that his body will be bundled away, hurriedly, in a borrowed grave, and so she performs in advance the ritual of death, so that he may know he is honoured, understood and cared for in death. Jesus says of the woman that 'wherever the good news is proclaimed in the whole world, what she has done will be told in remembrance of her'. All the indications are that she was enough in tune with the mission of Jesus not to mind that her story is so garbled. She is not the point of this action, Jesus is.

Luke 7: 36–50 has a very similar incident, in a different geographical and temporal setting. Luke's theological focus is different, too. The woman is identified as a sinner, and her action is more intimate and more degrading. She pours the oil on Jesus' feet, and wipes it with her hair, continuing to sob and to kiss his feet as the onlookers smirk, deriding both her and Jesus. 'If this man were a prophet, he would have known who and what kind of woman this is who is touching him – that she is a sinner' (Luke 7: 39). These self-satisfied people are very sure of the proper categories: to them it is inconceivable that Jesus might know all about the woman and still permit her to touch him.

In response to this, Jesus tells a story of forgiveness. Two debtors are both let off their debt, but the one who owed more is more grateful; this sinful woman is demonstrating the depth of her gratitude, as she receives forgiveness from Jesus. His hearers are clearly annoyed, offended and baffled in equal measure. He has made them look foolish, with a simple story of everyday debt; he has claimed the divine power to forgive sins; and he has subtly suggested that the woman is superior to them, in that she has recognized her indebtedness and responded with extravagant gratitude.

The theme of self-recognition comes up several times in Jesus' teaching, often with the underlying hint that religion and power can be used to bolster our self-deceit. Luke 18: 9–14 tells the story of the Pharisee and the tax collector, with the introduction: 'He also told this parable to some who trusted in themselves that they were righteous and regarded others with contempt.' The Pharisee lists his credentials to God, as one man of the world to another, while the tax collector simply says: 'God, be merciful to me, a sinner!' One puts his trust in himself and his achievements, and the other trusts in God alone.

This seems to be at the heart of some of the conflict between Jesus and the religious authorities of his day. The people who were confident that they had kept religious rules, and who were comfortable in the approval of their neighbours as a result, deeply resented Jesus' suggestions that religious rules are intended to set people free to live respectfully and healthily together, rather than to suggest that God is on the side of the respectable. Jesus takes as his campaign motto a quotation from the prophet Isaiah: 'The Spirit of the Lord is upon me, because he has anointed me to bring good news to the poor. He has sent me to proclaim release to the captives and recovery of sight to the blind, to let the oppressed go free, to proclaim the year of the Lord's favour' (Luke

4:18–19). This is what God's 'favour' looks like; whereas the self-righteous had assumed that God's favour is very like human favour – it is extended to those who keep on the right side of God, rather than those who need God.

From this understanding of God's action, Jesus came into conflict, over and over again, with those who saw the Law as a 'system', rigged in favour of those lucky enough to be able to be respectable. Jesus healed people on the sabbath, forgave people their sins, mixed with the unclean, ate with sinners, all the time enacting the boundary-crossing nature of God's power. God does not have to stay within safe, neat tramlines for fear that the divine holiness will be compromised. There is nothing that can make God unholy, so Jesus is able to take the cleansing power of God into all those situations of human mess and sinfulness, with no fear of what will happen to himself, no danger of contamination by what he encounters.

It is an evasion to read these encounters as a condemnation of a particular set of religious people or a rejection of the whole of the religious law of Judaism. Such a reading has been the source of appalling anti-Semitism and ludicrous misunderstanding of the living, relational covenant between God and human beings that is encapsulated in the Law. It has also been a form of exactly the kind of self-deceit that Jesus was attacking, in that it is based on assuming that 'we' are on the right side of God and 'others' are not. Jesus' actions seem to suggest that there is no safe place of our own making and no reliable way of determining who is 'in' with God and who is 'out'; anyone relying on religion or power or money as a form of certainty that does away with the necessity of dependence on God is missing the point, and that seems to be why those who have nothing else to depend upon find themselves instantly at home with the merciful humility of God. It makes space for them as no human systems do; it gives them a value that is based in the one who does the valuing, God, rather than in what the person being valued can put forward in their own defence.

Jesus' challenge to those who rely on wealth as a form of safety is just as stringent as to those who rely on set religious forms. The disciples are shocked by Jesus' lack of respect for the wealthy. For example, when he says, 'it is easier for a camel to go through the eye of a needle than for someone who is rich to enter the kingdom of God' (Matthew 19: 24), that is such a fundamental challenge to their understanding of power that they can hardly believe it. They had assumed, without question, that wealth and status were signs of God's approval, and underlying that is the unexamined belief that all wealth and status is of the same kind, so that God is, somehow, part of the ruling elite.

The rich young ruler is afraid that that might not be true. He comes to Jesus, perhaps hopeful that he will win commendation, yet uncertain enough to ask. Perhaps it is this uncertainty that Jesus sees with love (Mark 10: 21), but his response is uncompromising. The one thing that stands between Jesus and the young man is his wealth, because it offers the young man a security and certainty that mean that he feels he has choices; he does not feel an overwhelming need of Jesus, because his wealth muffles him in false security. He is the one who provokes Jesus' sad remark about the camel and the needle's eye.

Jesus tells the parable of the rich man, secure in his successful harvest, but unprepared for the fact that death is no respecter of wealth (Luke 12: 20), or of the rich man and Lazarus (Luke 16: 19–31), or of the widow's mite (Luke 21: 1–4); he enacts parables, such as putting a child in front of his disciples, and suggesting that this vulnerable and economically unproductive thing is what we must emulate, as the greatest example of the citizens of God's kingdom (Matthew 18: 1–5); he teaches that the first shall be last and the last shall be first (Mark 10: 31; Matthew 19: 30, 20: 16; Luke 13: 30). The Beatitudes (Matthew 5: 1–12, Luke 6: 20–23) encapsulate this revolution of understanding: the value structures of our everyday world do not correspond in any way to those of God. The least influential, the poorest, those least comfortably at home with the usual order of things, are seen to be the ones God values most because they need God most. Nothing encourages them to the self-deceit that the world is all right as it is.

According to John's gospel, on the night before he died, and in the full knowledge of what was to come, Jesus himself enacted a parable of the humility of God by washing his disciples' feet. Peter voices the shock of all the disciples as he exclaims: 'Lord, are you going to wash my feet?' (John 13: 6). Peter's reaction is natural – Jesus is performing the work of a slave, drawing water, washing filthy, hardened feet, wiping them dry; Peter assumes that he and all the disciples should reject this service, and call someone else to do it. He assumes that he is demonstrating understanding of Jesus' authority by questioning this action. But Jesus' response is not to allow Peter to take over this menial task but to challenge Peter to accept Jesus' service: 'Unless I wash you, you have no share with me' (John 13: 8). Peter must accept the tender, humble service of Jesus, both there, as Jesus washes his feet, and, even more, on the next day, when Jesus offers up his life. There is nothing that Peter or anyone else can offer to do instead of Jesus; they can only accept, with gratitude. The offer is there, even for Judas, though Jesus already knows that Judas is in league with his enemies. This service is not dependent on the merits of the disciples, but on the willingness of Jesus.

John's gospel is clear that Jesus does this out of the fullness of his power, 'knowing that the Father had given all things into his hands' (John 13: 3). As he explains the enacted parable to the disciples, he says: 'You call me Teacher and Lord – and you are right, for that is what I am' (John 13: 13). This is what the power of God looks like in action – it serves and cares for others. All of Jesus' challenging teaching, all of his ministry to the sick and the outcast, all of his confrontational interaction with those in power, is summed up here – the revolutionary power of God. God cannot be stopped because there is nothing God wants or needs from us; there is nothing we have that God requires; and so God has the utter freedom to offer us the divine love and service, if we will have it on those free terms, and not feel that it cannot be valuable unless we have in some sense bought it ourselves.

It seems the hardest thing for us to accept. Like Peter, we keep trying to persuade God not to be so humble, perhaps because it relativizes our own efforts so ruthlessly. Everything we earn and achieve will get us nowhere, as we meet God face to face, and all we will have to trust in is the reality of God, wearing the face of Jesus, and waiting to wash our feet. That is terrifying, because we find it so hard to believe that God does not know we are more important than our neighbour; but it is also the certainty of mercy, because it depends only on the character of God.

The Reformers called it 'justification by grace through faith', and even the faith is not ours, but Christ's. We may respond to that grace, freely offered, provided we do not then begin to imagine that our response is the cause of the grace. The only 'cause' is God, the mighty, the humble, the merciful.

ST FRANCIS OF ASSISI

Jesus' words to the rich young ruler, 'go and sell what you own and give the money to the poor', were certainly directed to one individual: Jesus did not say this to everyone he met, and so it is easy to hope that Jesus sensed in this young man some particular attachment to wealth that formed a barrier to his relationship with God, and that we do not need to assume that the same will be true for all of us. But at least some others have heard those words as addressed directly to them: among them, Francis of Assisi.

Francis was born in 1181 or 1182 to a wealthy family. His father was a well-travelled silk merchant, and Francis grew up in comfort. He was an attractive and lovable young man, always at the centre of a group of riotous friends, full of energy and a romantic longing to be involved in battles and acquit himself with honour. He got his wish, and spent some time as a prisoner of war, as a result.

Francis' change of life did not happen all at once; it seems to have had several stages. From his youth, he seems to have had a carefree attitude to wealth, which showed itself to begin with in his lavish and generous spending, and then found its true freedom when Francis renounced wealth altogether. Illness seems to have played a part in his change, too, as his biographers record a period of illness after his release from imprisonment, when the good things of life seemed to have lost all their savour, as though they had nothing in themselves to offer. 'But neither the beauty of the fields, the pleasantness of the vineyards, nor anything that is fair to see could in any wise delight him.'[1] He began to wonder if he had been misjudging things all his life.

Francis' first unmistakeable vision of God was enigmatic, leaving him confused and uncertain. His first biographer, Thomas of Celano, recounts the vision that Francis had when setting off to join in another war: he saw in a dream a room full of the accoutrements of war, and knew that they were for him and his knights to use in battle. But much as he tried to persuade himself that this dream was a portent of success in the coming fight, somehow he knew that was not true; instead of carrying on with his journey to join up, he went home, and began to search more determinedly for lasting, satisfying treasure.[2]

While praying in a dilapidated little church, Francis heard Jesus Christ speaking to him, instructing

[1] https://archive.org/stream/livessfrancisasoohowegoog#page/n28/mode/2up
[2] https://archive.org/stream/livessfrancisasoohowegoog#page/n30/mode/2up

him: 'Rebuild my church.' At first Francis took this command completely literally, and rushed off home to grab some supplies from his father's silk warehouse, sell them and give the proceeds to the startled priest of the little church of St Damiano. Unsurprisingly, his father was very angry, and eventually dragged Francis before the local bishop, demanding the return of his money, and threatening to disinherit Francis completely. Francis' response was to comply gladly, going even further than his father had intended by handing over every stitch of clothing he was wearing at the time.

From this time on, Francis took to a life of radical poverty and dependence. He ate if people fed him, and not otherwise; he slept outside more often than not. Despite its obvious hardships, Francis' life filled him with a joy that was tangible, and as he wandered the roads, preaching the good news of Jesus Christ, many heard him and he gained followers, to the extent that he had to begin to formalize their life together a little and write a rule, that was later developed by others.

Thomas of Celano's biography comes back, over and over again, to Francis' joy. He describes the attentive love with which Francis viewed nature: he loved sheep and lambs in particular, as symbols of the 'lamb of God'; he picked up worms and put them safely where they would not be trodden on;[3] he made sure that bees had honey or wine to feed on in cold weather so that they did not die; he loved flowers and preached to them, as he did to the birds, trusting that they, too, were sharers in the good news. This ecstatic love of nature is in direct contrast to the listless lack of pleasure in everything that beset him after his illness and before his conversion. It is as though God gave Francis back the deepest riches, once Francis realized that only God can give what belongs only to God.

Towards the end of his life, Francis had a vision of a crucified seraph, a strange and puzzling sight, on which he pondered long and hard.[4] As he did so, he noticed that the marks of crucifixion began to appear on his own body – the marks of the nails in his hands and feet, and the half-healed scar, as though a sword had once pierced his side.[5] Thomas writes that Francis never deliberately showed these marks to anyone, but that, in his final illness, while he was dependent

[3]https://archive.org/stream/livessfrancisasoohowegoog#page/n102/mode/2up/search/worm

[4]https://archive.org/stream/livessfrancisasoohowegoog#page/n116/mode/2up/search/seraph

[5]https://archive.org/stream/livessfrancisasoohowegoog#page/n136/mode/2up/search/nails

on others, he could not wholly conceal them, and after his death, several of the brothers saw them on his body.

Francis' hard physical life of frequent semi-starvation and exposure to the elements took its inevitable toll, and he died in 1226, still only in his forties. Before his death, his followers and the Church hierarchy had decided that Francis was not suitable to run what had become a large and influential movement. Such a significant thing could not rely just on Francis' example and the simple rule that Francis had first devised. Typically, Francis seems not to have minded about this at all. He handed over control of the order without any demur.

On his deathbed, Francis sang songs of praise to death, which he saw not as an enemy, or something to be feared, but as the means of entering into a new life. He also asked his friends to read to him from John's gospel, the passage which leads into the account of Jesus washing his disciples' feet.

Francis' legacy lives on, perhaps most compellingly in the strange intersection of love of poverty and glory in the beauty of nature. Despite its obvious hardships, Francis' life was not one that gloried in asceticism for its own sake, but he heard and believed that only God can truly satisfy the longings of the heart. While we are reliant for all essential sustenance on something that is not God, the deepest fulfilment will be denied us, because we have been prepared to settle for the safer, less satisfying, nourishment.

Francis' life was marked by the most outrageous humility. As he began, unintentionally, to grow one of the most influential renewal movements the Church has ever known, Francis always offered complete loyalty to bishops and to the Pope, never once imagining that he might challenge them. When his movement grew too big for him to be a direct presence with every follower, he handed over control with no stipulations. He lived a life of completely unselfconscious humility, which is still attractive and powerful to this day.

Perhaps Francis' most important legacy for our age is that humility is joyful. When Francis was living as though he was the centre of the world, somehow nothing was very meaningful. But when he abandoned everything to depend on God alone, the world became a place of piercing, ecstatic beauty. Everything became valuable in its own right, and able to offer up its loveliness, not as a commodity but as a gift.

Francis did not set out to found a new movement under his name, but to discover true joy, and he found it in humility, in poverty, chastity and obedience, the last places where most of us would look for joy. Francis' authority, like, Jesus', sprang from his dependence. And there is the challenge of Lent.

SUGGESTED RESPONSES

- Start each morning of Lent by hearing God say to you: 'You are my beloved.'
- Read the account of the calling of the disciples: Mark 1: 16–20:

  As Jesus passed along the Sea of Galilee, he saw Simon and his brother Andrew casting a net into the sea – for they were fishermen. And Jesus said to them, 'Follow me and I will make you fish for people.' And immediately they left their nets and followed him. As he went a little farther, he saw James son of Zebedee and his brother John, who were in their boat mending the nets. Immediately he called them; and they left their father Zebedee in the boat with the hired men, and followed him.

- If you were starting a new movement, how would you set about recruiting?
- What do you think Zebedee thought about it?
- How do you choose your friends?
- Thomas of Celano describes Francis' joy: when did you last feel 'joy', and why?

FURTHER READING ON FRANCIS

Thomas of Celano's biography is readily available online, for example at: https://archive.org/details/livessfrancisasoohowegoog

St Bonaventure also wrote a biography of St Francis: Tan Books, 2010.

Nikos Kazantzakis, *St Francis*, Loyola Classics, 2005. (This is a novel about St Francis' life.)

4

REIGNING FROM THE TREE

Lent prepares us to face Holy Week with Jesus. We have walked with him from his humble birth to his decisions in the wilderness, and watched those decisions being put into action in his ministry. Now the time of inevitable reckoning comes. Readers of the gospels have the great advantage of hindsight. The gospels are written and read in the light of the resurrection, with the knowledge that this story is about God's triumphant dealing with the world to set it free. The temptation is to rush to the end of the story, and so to miss the gospels' insistence that only *this* story leads to the resurrection. It is the man Jesus – who was loved and misunderstood in equal measure, and was ultimately rejected and abandoned, horribly executed by the Empire – this is the man, the only one, whom God has raised from the dead. There is no way to glory and new life except through the way of God's humility in Jesus Christ.

It is easy to marvel at the blindness and stupidity of those around Jesus, even his closest friends, who hoped in him when the crowds followed and cheered, but doubted and ran away when it looked as though his mission was coming to a humiliating end. We who live with God's unexpected response to the death of Jesus know that Jesus' mission was not a failure. But that does not mean that we now extrapolate from the action of God in Jesus' case to the characteristic action of God in other places. Jesus' story has a 'happy ending', which allows us to turn away from the necessary path of Jesus' life and death. In other words, we make exactly the same mistake as Jesus' contemporaries: in the light of the 'success' of the resurrection, we are willing to believe, but we do not want to hear, any more than they did, that there is no way to this end that does not walk with Jesus on the road to the Cross.

Part of the discipline of Lent is to open our imaginations to Jesus, and to commit to spending time with him, walking the path that he chose to walk, to discover its truth and strange power. From birth, through those choices in the wilderness, with his odd collection of friends around him, Jesus chooses the humble path that leads to the events of

Holy Week and to the Cross. The gospel witness is that this is the way of the Son of God in the world, and so it is paradigmatic for us. As we attend to Jesus, we are learning the shape of God's action, so that we can begin to trace it in our lives and in our world.

The gospels show the mounting tension of Jesus' mission, to the point where it is clear where it must end. Jesus has so many opportunities to back down, to walk away from the final confrontation, but only if he is willing to deny the truth of all that has gone before. The temptations in the wilderness are presented over and over again during Jesus' ministry: he could use his power for his own ends, for example. Luke 23: 8–9 shows Jesus taken to Herod's palace, as part of the build-up to his execution. 'When Herod saw Jesus, he was very glad, for he had been wanting to see him for a long time, because he … was hoping to see him perform some sign.' Perhaps Jesus could have bought his own safety by performing for Herod, but this would have acknowledged Herod's power, his right to give or withhold judgement; it would have reinforced the power structures of the world. So Jesus is silent in front of Herod, as God's devastating humility confronts Herod's worldly power. Herod cannot make the vulnerable man in front of him play by his rules.

John's gospel is the most explicit about the fact that the Cross is the ultimate sign of the power and action of God. John has the ironic motif of the 'glory' of God, hidden in plain sight in Jesus. Its manifestation is so unexpected in form that people are not able to recognize it. In John 1: 14, we read: 'we have seen his glory, the glory as of a father's only son.' This is what God's glory looks like: a relationship of love so strong that it gives total definition to Jesus. He will do nothing that does not flow from that relationship, because he is the Father's only Son. This is the glory that Jesus' followers are offered – a share in that eternal relationship. John 1 describes the creativity of the relationship between the Father and the Son, from which overflowing love all the world comes into being; and yet the world and its people are largely blind to their own reality: 'the world did not know him' (John 1: 10). 'Glory' is not recognized as flowing from our relatedness to the Father, through the work of the Son.

The theme of the glory between Father and Son comes up several times in John's gospel. There is a difficult exchange in John 8: 31ff between Jesus and some of his challengers, who are seeking to understand Jesus. The debate is all about family relationships. Jesus' interlocutors are claiming that their primary self-definition is as the children of Abraham, and that this gives them dignity and prestige. But Jesus counters them by saying that children are more interested in giving honour to their parents than in gaining what their parents have to give. 'I do not seek my own glory', he says. 'If I glorify myself, my glory is nothing' (John 8: 50, 54).

This relational glory flows out through the Holy Spirit, too. In John 16: 13–15, Jesus says that the virtuous circle from Father to Son will continue through the Holy Spirit to the disciples: 'He will glorify me, because he will take what is mine and declare it to you.'

'Glory' is found in relating, in the unbreakable witness of Son, Father and Spirit to the reality that everything flows from love. This is too simple to be credible. It is so simple that it becomes obscure and baffling. Even more baffling is John's insistence that the Cross is the most obvious and visible manifestation of the glory of Jesus' power. John 3: 14, 8: 28 and 12: 32 all speak of Jesus being 'lifted up', 'exalted', on the Cross, and in each case this enigmatic statement comes in the context of a statement or discussion about the relationship between Father and Son. Indeed, John 3: 14 is followed by the famous: 'For God so loved the world that he gave his only Son' (John 3: 16). Somehow, the Cross is the power of the merciful humility of God, hidden in plain sight. Here, if we could only see it, is the origin of the universe, in the unbreakable love of the Father and the Son.

Throughout the gospels, but particularly in Holy Week, the crowds, the authorities, and Jesus' own friends see and yet fail to see what is right in front of them.

The women disciples seem to have been the most prepared for Jesus' death. Perhaps they had the most reason to be wise about the way of power in the world, having suffered from it most constantly. The gospels are at one in their testimony that it was the women who were able to stay within sight of the Cross and watch to see where Jesus' body was laid. They had spices and ointments laid by, ready to perform the last rites for his abused body. The women did not see the Cross as the power of God at work to revolutionize the world: they just saw it as business as usual. They loved Jesus, and were grateful for all that they had received from him, in terms of healing, friendship, respect. But they thought that this, like all relationships, was temporary. Love is not the eternal reality of the world, just a passing respite from the merciless cycle of birth and death. So Mary Magdalene stands, weeping, in a garden, because the dead body of Jesus has been taken away (John 20: 11). John tells us that, even in the presence of the angels in the empty tomb, Mary can only see painful partings.

Peter, too, cannot see the truth of what is going on in front of him. Peter was part of the inner circle, among the very first to give up everything to follow Jesus. Peter saw something in Jesus that enabled him to declare: 'You are the Messiah' (Mark 8: 28), but he also had his own natural, preconceived notions about a Messiah. Immediately after Peter's bold vote of confidence, Jesus begins to explain to the disciples that his calling is going to lead to death, and Peter feels he has to correct him. As far as Peter is concerned, the Messiah is a victorious warrior, and Peter has no doubt what victory looks like. Jesus' response to Peter is so harsh that it is clear that some part of Jesus must wish that Peter was right: 'Get behind me, Satan! For you are setting your mind not on divine things but on human things' (Mark 8: 33). In all innocence, Peter has presented Jesus with the wilderness temptation again – choose power and safety or choose to be the Son of the Father.

Presumably, Peter must have told this story himself, as he must also have told about what happened on the night before Jesus died, since in each case there were no other witnesses likely to repeat what they saw. Peter, with his usual bravado, declares: 'Even though all become deserters, I will not' (Mark 14: 29). When Jesus is arrested, Peter follows, right into the courtyard of the High Priest's house. It is not clear what Peter thinks he can do, or whether he is still expecting Jesus to call out an army, even at the eleventh hour. If so, fear and reality quickly take over. Faced with the overwhelming evidence that Jesus is not going to fight or be rescued, Peter suddenly realizes his own vulnerability, and denies all knowledge of Jesus, when he is questioned.

'Peter' is a nickname, given by Jesus. Matthew 16: 17–20 seems to suggest that Jesus renamed Peter 'the Rock' after his confession of Jesus as the Messiah, and that it indicates confidence in Peter as a strong foundation for the Church; this is a very different outcome from the one reported in Mark's gospel. While there is no scholarly consensus about who wrote the letter 1 Peter, if it did have a close association with the apostle Peter, the play on the 'Rock' theme in 1 Peter 2 becomes particularly moving. 'Come to him, a living stone, though rejected by mortals yet chosen and precious in God's sight' (1 Peter 2: 4). It is as though the author is deliberately denying any suggestion that a human 'Peter the Rock' could ever be a firm foundation, because he, like everyone else, rejected Jesus, the only true foundation.

The story of the confession of Jesus as Messiah and the desertion of Jesus in the High Priest's courtyard must have been part of the testimony of Peter in later years, when he came to see how he had misunderstood the power of Jesus, hidden in plain sight. Peter described his own expectation of what success and power look like, and his inability to live up to his own standards. He stumbled when he tried to be most 'Rock-like', most 'Petrine', and the risen Jesus came to meet him in his humiliation. It is then that Peter truly became the Rock for others that his name implies.

If the women disciples missed the truth because their expectations were too low, and Peter missed it because he interpreted strength and success in conventional ways, the ordinary people of Jerusalem also missed it, as did Pilate, the governor.

The crowds swirl around Jesus throughout his ministry, sometimes interested, sometimes not. They liked it when he fed them (Matthew 14: 13–21, Mark 6: 30–44, Luke 9: 12–17); they found some of his teaching exciting, particularly when it provoked the authorities, who were anxious not to stir them up further: 'they were afraid of him, because the whole crowd were spellbound by his teaching' (Mark 11: 18); they loved the bustle and excitement of the triumphal entry into Jerusalem (Mark 11: 8–10). They, like Jesus' disciples, had all the evidence of Jesus' authority in teaching and healing, and they also noticed that he was using it strangely, not to ingratiate himself with the powerful, but to draw in the ordinary people. But they assumed, as did Peter and the others, that Jesus was challenging the particular religious and secular authorities of his day, rather than that Jesus was setting out a new interpretation of authority altogether. When the crowds realized that Jesus, like so many before him, was going to be defeated by the sheer power of the entrenched authorities, they lost interest in him. They joined in the mocking and spitting, and they called for his death (Mark 15: 12). For the crowd, Jesus had become just one more confirmation of the fact that nothing ever changes. He had seemed to be standing up for their rights, but he had failed.

Jesus' interaction with Pilate is intriguing, not least because it is Jesus who seems to have the freedom although Pilate has all the power. The edgy conversations between Jesus and Pilate that the gospels outline suggest that power is at the heart of Pilate's concerns. Jesus is brought to him as someone claiming to be 'king' (Mark 15: 2, Matthew 27: 11, Luke 23: 3, John 18: 33). Pilate's own authority belonged in a precarious pyramid of power, and he could not afford to let unrest in Judea get out of hand, since that would have provoked a large armed response from the Roman authorities, marching in to replace Pilate with more direct rule. When at last Pilate gives the order for Jesus' execution, his supposed claim to power is nailed up over the Cross, to make it clear that he died for daring to challenge Roman might. Even here, Pilate unknowingly tells the truth: the notice that he has put up over the Cross reads: 'Jesus of Nazareth, the King of the Jews'. When some protest at this apparent affirmation of Jesus' claim, Pilate simply says: 'What I have written, I have written' (John 19: 19–22).

Pilate never pretended to believe the charges against Jesus, and the gospels agree that he would have let Jesus go, if he could have done so without danger to his own position. But he could not. Jesus is free to answer or be silent, but Pilate has no such freedom: he must be seen and heard to do the right thing. Pilate with his armies is constrained, as Jesus is not. John's gospel plays with these ideas: when Pilate asks: 'Are you the King of the Jews?', Jesus replies: 'My kingdom is not from this world' (John 18: 33, 36). Implicitly, Jesus is claiming kingship, but not of a kind that Pilate can understand or defeat. As Jesus explains, if his own followers rose up and fought, Pilate and the Roman armies could defeat them, but they cannot defeat the truth to which Jesus testifies. The man facing death and the man ordering it look at each other, and it is Pilate who capitulates and acknowledges that he has no power to act freely.

There are two people who seem to grasp what is going on as Jesus goes to his death: one is a Roman centurion and the other a thief.

The centurion was presumably on duty, keeping an eye on the crowd, in case of trouble. If he was typical of his kind, he would have seen war in many parts of the Roman Empire, and been part of the brutally successful imperial machine that kept the diverse tribes and faiths under Roman rule. Mark gives us no clue as to what the centurion perceived, only its result: 'Now when the centurion, who stood facing him, saw that in this way he breathed his last, he said, "Truly this man was God's Son!"' (Mark 15: 39).

Jesus' last words had been the cry of dereliction: 'My God, my God, why have you forsaken me?' There is no reason to suppose that the centurion knew the end of the psalm, which affirms God's dominion over the nations, and even his dominion over the dead (Psalm 22: 27, 29). Jesus, who certainly would have known the psalm well, nevertheless chose the haunting opening verses, not the uplifting final ones, on which to end his earthly life.

What the centurion saw was a man willing to die for the reality that he called 'God', and, even in death, to call out to God. If God had indeed abandoned him, still Jesus did not curse God; even at this point, Jesus is questioning, expecting a response, perhaps. The centurion must have seen worse, must have had to abandon dying colleagues, some of them loyal to the Empire right to the end, some of them cursing the day they joined the army. Perhaps the centurion realized that the last name on the lips of a dying man is the name he loves most: even in death, Jesus turns to the Father. The only way in which this story can have come down to the later Christian community is if the centurion told it himself. Did he become a follower of the crucified Son of God? Did he come to acknowledge a different power, the power of the king who reigns from the tree?

The other person who sees Jesus' death not with fear or hatred or derision is the thief who hangs beside Jesus, under the same sentence of execution. While one criminal is mocking Jesus, saving his dying breath to taunt a fellow sufferer, the other thief asks: 'Do you not fear God?' (Luke 23: 40). He acknowledges his own punishment to be just, and he expects to face a higher court than the Roman one that hung him on the Cross: he expects to face God. He knows Jesus to be innocent. Perhaps he is hoping that when they both come before the judgement throne, Jesus will speak up for him. In that, of course, he is more correct than he can possibly imagine.

What the thief has somehow intuitively grasped is that human judgement is not final, and that in God's judgement, innocence and gentleness have power. Instinctively, he connects Jesus with the judgement of God, in a way that gives him comfort, and even hope.

In this new kingdom, where God judges, different rules apply.

As we travel through the gospel accounts of Jesus' arrest, trial and death, it is so very hard to see with the eyes of either the centurion or the thief. It is hard to see this as anything other than the usual power structure of the world asserting itself. The Cross breaks apart all our previous understandings of God, and confronts us with the reality of how God acts, as opposed to the fantasy of how we would act if we were God. The Cross is the heart of the merciful humility of God.

Matthew (27: 51), Mark (15: 18) and Luke (23: 45) all write that, as Jesus died, the veil of the Temple was torn in half. The veil served to protect the Holy of Holies from sacrilegious intrusion, and also to protect the world from the fearful presence of God. Only the High Priest ever entered behind the veil, and then only once a year, with elaborate ceremonies of purification, to offer sacrifices for the nation's sin in front of the Mercy Seat on the Ark of the Covenant. Now that protective veil was ripped away, and God's holiness was running amok. God was refusing to stay in holy isolation any more, and the whole system of dealing with sins was called into question, through the death of Jesus. As Jesus dies, the world order changes for ever, by the act of God. The thief was right to associate Jesus with judgement, and the centurion was right to see his death as the supreme act of obedience to the relationship between Father and Son.

All of this happens with Jesus' death. It does not wait for the glorious resurrection. Jesus accepts the world's judgement, and that puts an end to it. We have judged God, assuming in our arrogance and fear that we had that power. Now we wait, trembling, to see what the new order looks like, when we realize that the one we have crucified is the measure, the judge, the standard. We have done everything we can think of, and our resources are exhausted. The humble God has relentlessly absorbed all our cruelty, violence, hopelessness, selfishness and fear, never returning like for like, but carrying it away with him into death. All that is left now is the action of God.

TERESA OF AVILA AND THE HUMILITY OF GOD

Teresa (1515–82) is primarily known as a writer of the life of prayer. She was also an innovative and intensely hard-working reformer, completely revolutionizing the Carmelite order along lines of poverty and prayer, and founding new monasteries all over Spain, both for women and for men. She had an unusual combination of gifts, as a person of profound contemplative prayer and yet also a brilliant and active administrator. At the heart of Teresa's calling was the rediscovery of the way of humility as the way of life.

Without her parents' permission, Teresa joined the Carmelite order in 1536, and quickly gained a reputation for holiness. Then she suffered a severe, near-terminal illness, as did both Julian of Norwich and Francis of Assisi, as we have seen. There seems to be something about the experience of complete helplessness and dependence, together with the unavoidable reality of death, which put life into a different perspective for all of them.

In Teresa's case, her illness lasted for several years, and her recovery coincided with a time of deep weariness and depression. As a young woman, she had found prayer sweet and satisfying, but now she gave up the practice of private prayer almost entirely, and when she did start again, she found it dry and effortful. While she was conscious of her own lack of deep connection to God during this time, others still treated her as a woman of holiness, able to give good counsel. Even her own father came to her for advice about his spiritual life, when she would have said she hardly had a spiritual life of her own. In later years, this experience of the mismatch between inner and outer perceptions made her cautious about pronouncing judgement on what is really going on in another person's soul.

It was an encounter with an image of the suffering, dying Christ that brought Teresa back to the point where she could again feel the loving presence of God in her prayers. She describes suddenly noticing a statue of the dying Jesus, which seemed to her to be looking at her with deep, patient love. His patient willingness to hang and suffer for Teresa, while she could hardly be bothered even to pray, pierced her heart. She writes in her autobiography: 'So great was my distress when I thought how ill I had repaid Him for those wounds that I felt as if my heart were breaking, and I threw myself down beside Him, shedding floods of tears and begging Him to give me strength once and for all so that I might not offend Him.'[1] She also writes: 'I think I must have made greater progress,

[1]http://www.carmelitemonks.org/Vocation/teresa_life.pdf, chapter 9 (trans. Alison Peers).

because I had quite lost trust in myself and was placing all my confidence in God.'[2] Teresa had come to a place of honest humility that enabled her to see the humble God, waiting for her.

For the rest of her life, despite the sublime heights of contemplative prayer that she reached, and the practices she taught to others, Teresa always insisted that we must not try to move away from the suffering humanity of Christ, or to feel that we are ready to dwell on the risen and ascended glorious Christ instead. The humanity of Christ remained the focus of all her prayer. Teresa was clear that we do not pray because it makes us feel good, or so that we may have wonderful mystical experiences. They come and go, as does insight and understanding. Our job is just to carry on praying. She describes the activity of prayer as 'like the little donkeys that draw the … waterwheel. Though their eyes are shut and they have no idea what they are doing, these donkeys will draw more water than the gardener can with all his efforts.'[3]

Up to this point, although Teresa had been living a celibate life of prayer, her circumstances were not

[2] Ibid.
[3] Ibid., chapter 22.

dissimilar to those of any well-off woman of her day. Her convent was comfortable, and she was able to come and go and have friends and visitors. Looking back over her period of dryness, she began to see that her way of life had contributed to her inability to find God, because it took any sense of urgency and reality from her call. She was living as though the ordinary things of the world were as real and important to her as God.

From this time, Teresa sought to reform her order, and draw it back to its original vision of a life of poverty and prayer, a way of life that could grow true dependence on God, because the other ephemeral and unreliable things that we are tempted to rely on were removed. She got permission to set up a new House, dedicated to St Joseph, that saint of the hidden, obscure life of obedience. Part of the struggle for this new foundation was that Teresa was determined not to accept endowments from wealthy patrons, who would then expect to have some stake in the convent, and whose wealth and influence would give a false security to the order. She wanted genuine poverty for her sisters. Over the years that followed, under considerable opposition and pressure, Teresa founded a number of new houses of the Discalced Carmelite order. 'Discalced' means 'shoeless', which described both literally and symbolically the poverty in which the new nuns and monks were to live, without the protection of wealth to cushion them from the strict reality of their calling.

Teresa's Spain was a place where rank and status were carefully measured and preserved. In the convent as she originally found it, it was still clear which nuns were highly born and which were not. In her new convents, Teresa put an unusual emphasis on friendship and equality. This seems to have come very directly from her communion with the suffering and humiliated Christ. Teresa often called God 'His Majesty', recognizing God's honour and the loyalty and devotion that God has the right to command from us. But instead, God's majesty is shown in what God will do for us, to bring us into his kingdom. For Teresa, it makes no sense to belong to the Majesty of God and yet to try to operate our own different standards. If this is how the King treats his subjects, then this is how those subjects must treat each other.

She writes of how weary we become when we fasten our desires on things that are worthless. Somehow, we are deceived into believing that worthless things are important, when all the time, it is clear that only the things of God can be of any lasting benefit: 'for what passes away, and is not pleasing to God, is worth nothing and less than nothing.'[4] She continues:

> What is there that can be bought with this money which people desire? Is there anything valuable? Is there anything lasting? If not, why do we desire it? ... Oh, if all would agree to consider it as useless dross, how well the world would get on, and how little trafficking there would be! How friendly we should all be with one another if nobody were interested in money and honour! I really believe this would be a remedy for everything.[5]

Teresa believed that life in community was a significant gift for keeping us humble. In particular, she noted the temptation for her Sisters to compare themselves with each other, in holiness, in contemplative prayer and so on. Recalling the days when others thought her holy when she knew herself to be empty of any wisdom or true connection with God, Teresa counselled against judging what is going

[4]Ibid., chapter 20.
[5]Ibid.

on between another Christian and God. Our calling is to remain faithful, which we can only do if we are willing to be humble and dependent. She writes that God makes some people contemplatives, but that this is a gift, not a necessity for salvation, and not a badge of honour for the contemplative. If the gift is not given, 'consider yourself lucky to serve the servants of the Lord and praise His Majesty'.[6]

Teresa's writing is lively and insightful, full of good advice on the life of prayer. Essential to this is her honesty. Once, when she was under extreme pressure, she heard God saying that she must not worry, because this is a sign of God's friendship. She is reported to have replied: 'No wonder you have so few friends!' Yet she remained convinced that only constant companionship with the humble power of the human Jesus could bring true satisfaction. Whatever else we set our hearts and souls on will prove to be fleeting, unsatisfying and undependable. Only this God, who comes to find us, can fill our mundane lives with the joy of lasting friendship and trust.

[6]*The Way of Perfection,* trans. Kieran Kavanaugh and Otilio Rodriguez (ICS Publications, 1980), vol. 2, chapter 17, p. 99.

Teresa's reconversion through the image of the suffering Christ gave her the strength and motivation to challenge ways of life that do us harm, offering pleasure where there is none. God makes a home with us in Jesus so that we may indeed have a true home. God does not and will not do this by force, for an enforced home is an institution. God's divine patience is a limitless resource, making space for us, holding the door open, freely, but with such power that nothing but our own hand can shut it.

SUGGESTED RESPONSES

- Start each morning of Lent by hearing God say to you: 'You are my beloved.'
- Read the encounter between Jesus and Pilate; John 18: 33–38:

  Then Pilate entered the headquarters again, summoned Jesus, and asked him, 'Are you the King of the Jews?' Jesus answered, 'Do you ask this on your own, or did others tell you about me?' Pilate replied, 'I am not a Jew, am I? Your own nation and the chief priests have handed you over to me. What have you done?' Jesus answered, 'My kingdom is not from this world. If my kingdom were from this world, my followers would be fighting to keep me from being handed over to the Jews. But as it is, my kingdom is not from here.' Pilate asked him, 'So you are a king?' Jesus answered, 'You say that I am a king. For this I was born, and for this I came into the world, to testify to the truth. Everyone who belongs to the truth listens to my voice.' Pilate asked him, 'What is truth?'

- Notice how unafraid Jesus is: asking Pilate where he got his information; challenging Pilate's understanding of kingship.
- What do you make of Pilate's question: 'What is truth?'
- Are you aware of times in your life when you have sided with those in power, even if you were not really comfortable about that?
- Teresa of Avila found it important to look at a statue of Jesus on the Cross. Do you think this is a helpful practice?

FURTHER READING ON TERESA OF AVILA

E. Alison Peers' translation and edited edition of Teresa's
    Life can be found at: http://www.carmelitemonks.org/
    Vocation/teresa_life.pdf

Rowan Williams, *Teresa of Avila*, Continuum, 2004.

RISEN AND ASCENDED INTO HUMILITY

Through Lent, we follow Jesus on the path that leads from the temptation in the wilderness to his death. The journey starts at Jesus' baptism, with the voice of God the Father, speaking words of love and affirmation over Jesus, as the gentle presence of the dove-like Holy Spirit hovers over him. But then the dove turns into a driving force that impels Jesus into the wilderness to face the temptation to be the powerful and imperious Son of God, rather than the obedient and misunderstood Son of Man. From there, as we walk with Jesus, we meet his first followers: fishermen, tax collectors, women and nobodies. In an agony of frustration, we see him provoking and alienating the powerful, who might help him, and spending all his efforts of love and power on the useless. Finally, we come to the inevitable end of such a career, at a place of execution, where the powerful display what happens to those who do not know their place, who do not respect the proper structure of the world. Our Lent journey is one of painful attention, as we try to watch Jesus, and understand. This human being is the presence and action of God in the world; he is the clue to the character and meaning of God; he is the only one who has seen the Father (John 6: 46). Yet we, like those who met him on the roads of Palestine, cannot quite believe that Jesus has it right; there is so little of what we long for from God in this way of living and dying.

Then, at last, God behaves as we expect, and Jesus is raised from the dead. Yet even in this exhilarating display of force, that questions the very meaning of death, still there are those signs of God's mysterious and life-giving humility. The risen Jesus does not come to his enemies and force them to admit they were wrong and kneel before his transcendent aliveness; his risen body is not gleaming and burnished with the light that cannot be hidden. With one exception, the risen Jesus comes only to those who had been his friends and his followers before he died, and he comes with the marks of his suffering body still visible in the scars of the nails. Even to the one exception, St Paul, Jesus comes and declares himself one with the suffering, rather than the Lord of life and death. The resurrection undoes nothing of what Jesus has been up to his death; instead, the resurrection confirms the life of Jesus as the way of God in the world. After Pentecost, when the Holy Spirit comes upon Jesus' followers to give the courage and the words to witness, this is what Peter says to that first Pentecost crowd, as the good news of God's action: 'this man ... you crucified and killed ... But God raised him up, having freed him from death, because it was impossible for him to be held in its power' (Acts 2: 23–24). Telling the story of Jesus is what disciples have been called to do ever since. Although Jesus is alive, too mighty to be held by death, yet still he gives himself into our hands, and makes our words and our lives his only witnesses in the world.

The gospels are, as always, selective in their telling of the resurrection. Jesus is the full presence of God, fully living a human life, and yet so much of it was not noticed or recorded; and the same pattern persists in the resurrection narratives – a fully human life raised into the eternal life of God, and yet so few accounts of what happens when dying humanity and living humanity meet.

In the earliest manuscripts we have of Mark's gospel, no one meets the risen Jesus. Mark 16: 1–8 describes how a few women set out early on the Sunday morning, after the sabbath was over, to minister to the dead body of the man they had all loved, honoured and followed. They see the empty tomb, and 'a young man, dressed in a white robe, sitting on the right side' (Mark 16: 5). The man may or may not have been an angel – Mark does not comment on that. The man tells the women that Jesus – who was crucified – is raised from the dead. The emphasis on the reality of the crucifixion makes it clear that the young man is not saying that Jesus was not really dead and has now been resuscitated; this is something entirely different, and the women are charged with this message for Peter and the other disciples.

According to the oldest version of Mark's gospel, the women do not carry out their commission: 'they said nothing to anyone, for they were afraid' (Mark 16: 8). Mark does not say that the women disbelieved what the young man told them; but they could not tell others because they were terrified. They have no means of making sense of what they have been told. During Jesus' life, they may have hoped for a revolution, putting Jesus and his followers in charge of a more just and gentler world, where there might even be room for women to be heard and to flourish. But with Jesus' death, all of their hopes were at an end, and everything returned to normal; they were once again of no interest or value. A world in which Jesus and his ideals were really put to death by the powerful, but in which Jesus is now alive beyond death – such a world made no sense at all. The women had no means of telling what that might herald; they literally had no words for it. It certainly did not occur to them that this might be good and joyful news.

This is such a dark and baffling ending to the gospel, that other compilations of resurrection stories were quickly added, in verses 9–20 of chapter 16. The women pluck up courage and finally pass on the message they were given, although, predictably, no one believes them anyway. Then Mary Magdalene encounters the risen Jesus, but she is not believed either; neither were a couple who meet Jesus on the road. It is not until Jesus comes to all of the remaining eleven disciples that they finally accept the truth and cautiously realize that it is, indeed, good news. These slightly later additions to the gospel of Mark do preserve the sense of fear and puzzlement, acknowledging that the resurrection made no sense to begin with, and was certainly not immediately seen as a cause for rejoicing. It is hard to believe that Mark really meant to end his gospel at verse 8, with the women running away in terror and in silence: in the Greek in which the gospel is originally written, verse 8 is almost an incomplete sentence. All kinds of theories have been put forward, for and against this ending. But whatever the truth of the matter, what is striking is that the narrative creeps towards joy with painful, fearful caution.

Matthew's gospel has a slightly more conventional telling of the resurrection. It starts very much like Mark's, with a couple of women going sadly to visit Jesus' grave. In Matthew, it is very definitely an angel that they meet, accompanied by an earthquake and looking 'like lightning' (Matthew 28: 3). This time, the women agree to pass the message on to the other disciples, and although they are afraid, they are also beginning to be joyful, as they meet Jesus himself. But Matthew's gospel, too, has the mysterious undertone of doubt. Faced with the evidence of the full power of the life of God, the religious authorities quickly organize a conspiracy of lies about the resurrection, spreading the rumour that Jesus' disciples stole the body at night (Matthew 28: 11–15). The disciples themselves, when they finally meet the risen Jesus, have options about how they respond, and 'some doubted' (Matthew 28: 17). Even resurrection power is, apparently, humble power, not overwhelming its witnesses into submission, but inviting them to believe.

The gospels of Luke and John have fuller accounts of encounters with Jesus, risen from the dead. Luke starts with the familiar story of the women going to the tomb early in the morning, and meeting the terrifying truth of the empty tomb and the angelic messengers. The other disciples hear the women's witness as 'an idle tale' (Luke 24: 11). Peter follows it up by checking on the tomb, but Luke says that Peter was 'amazed' (Luke 24: 12), rather than joyful or converted, and there is no sign that Peter attempted to share what he had seen with the others: he had learned a lesson from their treatment of the women.

In Luke, the angelic messengers attempt to remind the women that Jesus had told them that his death was a necessary part of the story, not the end of it (Luke 24: 6–7); and the same theme is picked up in the meeting on the road to Emmaus. Two disheartened followers of Jesus meet a stranger and pour out their woes, the death of all their hopes: 'we had hoped that he was the one to redeem Israel', they say mournfully (Luke 24: 21). The stranger is wholly unsympathetic: 'Oh, how foolish you are, and how slow of heart to believe all that the prophets have declared!' (Luke 24: 25), he remarks, and then proceeds to take them through the scriptural evidence that should have enabled them to see the work of God in Jesus' death. Just as they were too stupid to see the witness of scripture, until it is pointed out to them, so they are too stupid to recognize their companion until the homely, familiar act of breaking bread opens their eyes. The action of God is hidden in plain sight, but because it is so different from our expectations, we, like the couple on the road to Emmaus, cannot even see it. For ever afterwards, we are going to need to keep returning to the scriptures, and the table where bread is broken, to keep checking that we have not slipped back into bad habits of failing to recognize the mighty humility of God.

The eleven disciples, when they, too, meet Jesus, risen from the dead, are similarly obtuse. They assume that Jesus must be a ghost, because that is the only frame of reference they can dredge up for such an occurrence (Luke 24: 37). Yet again, Jesus has to challenge their doubt, and lead them back to the scriptural witness to how God acts.

Luke's theological emphasis is very much on the continuity between Jesus' death and resurrection. The death of Jesus is not the strange aberration in the otherwise victorious story of the saving power of God. Instead, the death of Jesus is a necessary part of the story, without which the resurrection is not good news. It is because Jesus suffered and died that his resurrection commissions the disciples to proclaim 'repentance and forgiveness' in his name for ever more (Luke 24: 47). This is the good news that God holds the reality of our sinfulness and death in tandem with the divine reality of restoration and life. This is not good news that overrides bitter truth, or pretends it has no power, because that is make-believe, which cannot set us free. Instead, this is good news that takes the stuff of darkness and turns it inside out, making it tell a different story with a new ending. This is a story of God's telling, not just ours.

If Luke's resurrection narrative emphasizes the scriptural witness to the divine nature, John's emphasizes the fact that God, the eternal one, deals with each person individually. The story Luke tells is of the restoration of meaning to the whole world, and

John makes it clear that this is not solely a generic, universal narrative, but that restoration happens for each person, as they find that their life's story is given a new direction by Jesus, risen from the dead.

Mary Magdalene, weeping in the garden beside the empty tomb, hears again her name, spoken by the beloved voice (John 20: 16). Mary had thought she could only be herself with Jesus; only Jesus forgave her, trusted her, called her by name. Others saw her as a woman with a past that would always dictate her future, but Jesus had given her hope that her life might have a greater meaning. All of that had died with him, and so Mary weeps, publicly, with abandon, a woman who is used to being sneered at and judged, and expecting to resume that old course of her life. Instead, Jesus tells her that she no longer needs to cling to that one precious relationship from the past; the Mary she was in Jesus' presence is the Mary she truly is now and always. She is Mary the apostle, sent with good news, free and powerful.

Thomas, too, meets Jesus risen from the dead, so that Thomas' story, too, is no longer defined by the past but by what is to come. Thomas will not believe the testimony of the other disciples. He is curiously determined that he will only believe if he sees 'the mark of the nails in his hands, and put my finger in the mark of the nails and my hand in his side' (John 20: 25). Such detailed, emphatic insistence on what is necessary for Thomas to believe! It is as though Thomas suspects that the others have been duped by some person like Jesus, not really risen, because never really dead. Death is a fact that Thomas can understand; but resurrection? With infinite patience and even humour, Jesus comes to Thomas and gives him what he needs, so that Thomas can go out and convince others like himself, the ones who need the evidence that Thomas so desperately needed. Thomas the doubter becomes the very first person to name Jesus' divinity: 'My Lord and my God!' (John 20: 28).

Perhaps most moving of all is Jesus' meeting with Peter. The setting is a homely and familiar one, with fish cooking on a barbecue by the shore of the lake. Peter has decided to go back to the old ways; he was a fisherman when Jesus called him, and now that Jesus is dead, the bigger future he had begun to imagine for himself is nonsense, so Peter the fisherman is the only reality left.

When Peter realizes that he is about to meet Jesus, back from the dead, he does the strangest thing: he has been fishing naked, because fishing is wet and messy work, but as he prepares to meet the Lord, he puts all his clothes back on, and jumps into the water. It is such a human, revealing act. Peter is afraid of this meeting; the old, informal, trusting relationship with Jesus died, not just on the Cross; in Peter's mind, that relationship died when he, Peter the Rock, betrayed Jesus by the courtyard fire in the High Priest's grounds. Here, by another fire, he is going to meet Jesus again. Peter is brave – he rushes on towards Jesus, not waiting for the boat to come ashore, not giving himself time to think; but even so, he needs to have his clothes on to face what is to come.

Peter must be fearing anger and rebuke, demands for an explanation; or he might be hoping that dying has wiped it all out of Jesus' memory, and they can start again. But what he gets is neither: Jesus gives Peter the chance to remake the story of desertion, to own it as his own, but not the final truth about him. Peter denied Jesus three times, and now, three times, he is given the opportunity to affirm his love for Jesus. And so Peter the Rock becomes Peter the Shepherd. His courage and strength are to take a new form, and to be put to the service of the vulnerable, the needy, the dependant, the stupid. Peter can now walk in the merciful humility that Jesus has shown to him, and that he can show to others.

The incarnate Jesus lived at a particular time, in a particular place, and met real people. Jesus risen from the dead does not float off into divine abstraction, but still meets people as they actually are, and turns them around to tell a new story: the good news that God can bring life out of death, even the death of all hope and possibility; God can give our past a new future, and we know this, because the crucified one is risen.

Although the gospels each tell of meeting the risen Jesus from a slightly different point of view, there are recognizable common elements. For example, all agree that fear is the first reaction to the resurrection: resurrection is unexpected, and it is not immediately obvious that it bodes well for those still living towards death. The women who were the first witnesses are also common to all the gospels, as a clear sign of the continuing strangeness of God's action. The women could not be believed until the male disciples had also met Jesus, so it is hard to see why God bothered to display this miracle to them at all; unless God thought that their love and faithfulness deserved its reward, and that they, just like the male disciples, could tell the story of a new future for all humanity, male and female.

The gospels are also agreed that although the resurrection ought to be the most sublime display of divine power, it is not used to that effect. Jesus appears only to those who had known him before death, and only to those who had begun to hope and trust in him already. He does not confront those who put him to death, or make himself manifest to the wider world. Even his disciples do not always recognize him. This shockingly new life is still hidden, still available only as part of a relationship with Jesus, in his humanity, his suffering and his death. It obstinately refuses to be separated from that framework of explanation. When the disciples choose a twelfth to fill the place of the traitor, Judas, this is the criterion that they use: someone who was with Jesus 'beginning from the baptism of John until the day when he was taken up from us – one of these must become a witness with us to his resurrection' (Acts 1: 22). There must never be any temptation to tell the story of the resurrection or to try to guess its meaning apart from in the life and death of Jesus.

That criterion makes the final meeting between Jesus in the resurrection flesh and a human being particularly strange. Paul claimed that his meeting with Jesus on the road to Damascus was not a vision but a resurrection appearance. In 1 Corinthians 15, Paul is recounting the evidence for the resurrection, detailing the witnesses, so that his Corinthian readers will understand that the theology of the destruction of death through the resurrection power of Jesus Christ is not just theory, but based in fact. Paul does not mention the women, who might not help to persuade the Corinthians, but he mentions Peter, the Twelve, and a great many others, before writing: 'Last of all, as to one untimely born, he appeared also to me' (1 Corinthians 15: 8). Paul knows that this meeting is 'untimely', since it happens after the Ascension, but he is sure that it counts as a resurrection appearance. It is of such significance to the mission of the Jesus movement that it is described twice in Acts (Acts 9: 1–9; Acts 26: 9–19), and Paul mentions it himself, though without details, in Galatians 1: 13–16.

Jesus' appearance to Paul is unlike the other resurrection appearances; there is fierce light, so that Paul is blinded, and only hears Jesus, without seeing him. But despite the display of power, what Jesus says is very much in tune with the nature of Jesus as encountered in the gospels. Jesus asks: 'Why do you persecute me?' Paul is forced to understand the identification of Jesus with the ongoing suffering of his people; he has not removed himself from the memory of suffering, now that his glorious resurrection body is beyond pain and death.

However the appearance to Paul is interpreted, Paul becomes a worthy, indeed, vital, witness to the death and resurrection of Jesus. He rebuilds his life and teaching around 'God's foolishness' and 'God's weakness', which 'is stronger than human strength' (1 Corinthians 1: 25). Paul reminds all Jesus' followers that they – we – do not win their own salvation through strength, wit or merit, but through the merciful humility of God in Jesus Christ.

Paul and the gospels agree that there is a point after which the risen Jesus is not encountered in 'the flesh', even the transformed flesh that is no longer subject to death. The 'Ascension' is mentioned briefly in Mark and Matthew, and at greater length in Luke and Acts, and accompanied by the 'great commission', or the great promise of Jesus' continuing presence and faithful action through the disciples who witness to him, in the power of the Holy Spirit.

It is the letter to the Hebrews that most develops the theology of the Ascension. It is not just that

Jesus, the eternal Son of God, now returns home to his proper place and existence; it is also that Jesus, the obedient, suffering and risen human being, 'is seated at the right hand of the throne of the Majesty in the heavens' (Hebrews 8: 1). The two cannot be separated out. There is no access to the Son of God, or to the saving power of God, except through the person of Jesus of Nazareth. 'In the days of his flesh, Jesus offered up prayers and supplications, with loud cries and tears … Although he was a Son, he learned obedience through what he suffered' (Hebrews 5: 7–8). And this, according to Hebrews, is the source of our life. For ever, reaching back to the beginning of creation, and stretching forward to its consummation, there is no way round this story of the suffering Jesus, in whom heaven and earth are held together. Only Jesus, the Son who was willing to learn obedience through human suffering and death, has broken through death to pour God's life and forgiveness into the world.

That is why the apostles had to choose someone who could bear witness to the reality of the whole of Jesus' human life, from baptism to death and resurrection; that is why the Christian community has its central, defining acts, baptism and Eucharist, in which we tell and enact and enter into the death and life of Jesus

Christ. We leave behind our own interpretations of power and salvation, of achievement and merit, and step into the space made for us by the humility of God, so strong that death cannot overcome it.

The ascension of Jesus is not an unnecessary embellishment: it is the establishment of this one story, of this one man, as the way in which the character of God is known and followed. We must not universalize the story, and make it one of human and divine encounter; we must not look for the essential sacramentality of the whole universe, or the original, inalienable connection between creature and creator. We must just tell this story of Jesus Christ, as faithfully and humbly as our faithless and destructive pride will let us. The risen and ascended Lord still and always bears the marks of the nails. They are the source of our hope that what we cannot do for ourselves, in all our strength and arrogance, God can do, in the divine and merciful humility.

JEAN VANIER AND L'ARCHE

As a young man, Vanier joined the Royal Navy, spending eight years working on naval ships including during the Second World War. Many at that time viewed war as an essential way to bring peace, and Vanier was a young and idealistic sailor. Still only 21 by the time he left the Navy in 1950, Vanier was still searching for peace. He joined a small community near Paris, drawn to the mixture of prayer, manual labour and study in community. It was during this period that he first became aware of how people with disabilities were being treated, almost as though they were expendable, hardly human. He visited an institution, under the care of a Christian chaplain, and was touched to the core of his being.

He bought a small house and invited two disabled men to come and live with him. This was the birth of L'Arche movement, with family houses set up all over the world, and small communities of women and men, some with disabilities, some without, sharing life together.

For Vanier, the heart of this movement seems to be a profound meditation on what it is to be human. It is not just the people with disabilities who discover the dignity of being treated as human, it is also the so-called able who discover that there is an intrinsic worth to humanity that is nothing to do with achievement. He writes: 'it has been this life together that has helped me become more human. Those I have lived with have helped me to recognize and accept my own weaknesses and vulnerability.'[1]

What Vanier discovered, as he lived in community, was that there are profound lessons to be learned about our whole society and our own humanity when people of very different abilities live together. As a society, we have valued only certain gifts and abilities, the obvious ones of success that lead to power and the ability to control our lives and the lives of others. But the problem is that, however powerful and gifted an individual or an institution may be, life is not wholly controllable, so failure is inevitable. But since we do not value failure, that means we are constantly faced with the reality that we cannot be wholly valued. If we fail – and we all will – then we lose value. So an individual and corporate culture driven by the need to succeed is always also, implicitly, driven by the fear of failure and the lack of self-worth.

Vanier also reflects on the unacknowledged consequences for our world of an attitude that values only greater and greater power, control and 'success'. A society orientated towards 'success' will unwittingly discard the unsuccessful, demand more and more of

---

[1] Jean Vanier, *Becoming Human* (Paulist Press, 1998), kindle edition, loc. 51.

the earth's resources, and become gradually more and more dangerously exploitative and unequal. These are not the stated goals of a competitive and success-driven individual or culture, and so they are often not observed until terrible damage has been done. The earth's resources are depleted, and the poor and the powerless feel the effects of this first, because the world is run by the rich and the successful, in their interests. Since this is clearly not a sustainable state of affairs, the world grows increasingly violent and unstable, as the poor fight for life and the rich fight for control.

Vanier does not claim to be a politician, merely an observer of a microcosm of this world, as it is found in L'Arche communities. L'Arche is full of people who have been judged worthless and expendable, and also of people who have seen the unsustainability of a way of living that is so profligate with its human resources. In such communities, as Vanier discovered for himself, the essential, inalienable weakness of each human being can be faced without fear. 'Our lives are a mystery of growth from weakness to weakness.'[2] We start our lives as vulnerable children, and most of

[2]Ibid., loc. 486.

us end our lives moving through increasing infirmity towards death. Yet the rhetoric of our society gives us no way of valuing this fundamental truth, so we can only fear it.

The dominant social narrative of the present age is one of 'the survival of the fittest', but the same evolutionary narrative can perceive that groups and individuals that seek the common good are also more likely to survive. History is not univocal; we have choices about how we will interpret the forces that drive us.

One of the interpretive keys that Vanier uses to help us see different ways of exploring reality is what he calls 'the heart'. He writes: 'The heart is never "successful". It does not want power, honours, privilege, or efficiency; it seeks a personal relationship with another, a communion of hearts.'[3] But at the same time, the heart cannot fulfil its needs without opening itself to vulnerability. The 'communion of hearts' can never be achieved if personal safety and success come first. Nor is it easy to admit only one, trusted person into that place of vulnerability, for to admit what the heart needs is to critique a description

[3]Ibid., loc. 776.

of the world that does not prioritize that need. If we need such connection, then others do, too. To deny them the possibility of connection, even connection with us, is self-contradictory. People with disabilities do not have the choices that others sometimes believe they have. People with disabilities cannot avoid vulnerability and dependence, so must live in 'the way of the heart', where success and efficiency and power are not the main currency.

If we are to be true to this longing for connection, then we are challenged to see and honour that connection in others; we begin to see that others are human beings, with needs, with fears, with failings, with histories, just like our own. When Vanier is helping his audience to understand the meaning of L'Arche, he very often tells the stories of individuals, so that we come to see them not just as 'the disabled', but as Antonio, Claudia, Eric, Nadine.

God in Christ does the same. Jesus meets individuals and groups and interacts with them. God does not administer justice from on high, singling out 'the good' and 'the evil'. Instead, God hears the stories of each individual. In particular, Jesus chooses to hear and be part of the stories of those who are excluded and marginalized. He speaks with lepers and women and Samaritans; he heals the blind and the lame, and brings them back into the 'mainstream', by declaring in word and deed that their lives, their stories, also matter. Gradually, the gospels show us the world through Jesus' eyes, and it is bigger than his contemporaries thought, because it includes all the invisible people at the margins.

In one of the most profoundly helpful and challenging sections of *Becoming Human*, Vanier reflects on forgiveness as a necessary enlargement of our vision of the world, a necessary corollary to acknowledging the way of 'the heart'. Hatred of others, however justified, is a way of excluding them from the imaginative connection that 'the heart' urges upon us. One of Vanier's correspondents described to him how she had inherited her grandfather's hatred of the Germans because of his experience of the Second World War. Her story strikingly illustrates the long-term consequences of hatred: in her case, it shaped her family for several generations, and the same corrosive effect of hatred can be seen in groups and societies that accustom themselves to dehumanizing each other. The woman who wrote to Vanier describes the slow and painful process of liberation from the inter-generational hatred. She quotes a principle used by

Native Americans in their decision-making: 'Reflect on the consequences for the following generations.'[4]

It can seem like weakness to forgive, particularly if there is no guarantee that the other has admitted fault or will receive forgiveness. It opens up an area of vulnerability again. As Vanier writes, 'forgiveness is unilateral'.[5] It does not wait until it is sure of the response, or until both sides are equally vulnerable. The hope is that reconciliation follows on forgiveness, but even if it does not, forgiveness is freeing. To hate is to be shaped by what is hated; paradoxically, it gives power to what is hated to continue to shape life and choices. Hatred casts a long shadow, and draws others into its path, dictating their choices, too. Whereas forgiveness brings freedom and new possibilities.

This simple analysis gives immediate access to the logic of God's humility. The humble God makes the world bigger, because God's humility notices and includes those who do not fit the dominant narrative of the world. Those who will never be 'successful', as success is commonly measured, 'succeed' in being loved by God. Since, as Vanier points out, no one can

[4]Ibid., loc. 1734.
[5]Ibid., loc. 1721.

ever be wholly and always successful, we all need the mercy of the humble God, in our brokenness and failure. In our strength and power, we too can exercise the divine mercy, by using what we have to make the world bigger, to include more and more people in the narrative of what it is to be human.

Matthew 25: 31–46 tells the parable of the Sheep and the Goats. The 'sheep' are successful: they have opportunities and gifts, but they choose to use them to bring others into the fortunate circle. Through their actions, they tell a story of the equal value of all human beings, so that they are able to see need, recognize it as similar to their own, and respond as though those in need have a right to expect help. The 'sheep' do not do this for any reason, other than that they recognize their common humanity with the people in need. They are astonished to find that this is their true 'success' in God's eyes, because they were not thinking of success or failure at all, just connection with another human being. The 'goats', on the other hand, by denying the needs of others, were in effect treating the others as less than human, and were assuming that their own privilege was a proper reward for them, not something that required them to share.

Both sheep and goats discovered that human beings are made to be interdependent and vulnerable to each other, so that 'success' cannot be achieved by any at the expense of others. This is the reality that Vanier and L'Arche communities have discovered, and offer to us as a model.

SUGGESTED RESPONSES

- Start each morning of Lent by hearing God say to you: 'You are my beloved.'
- Read Jesus' encounter with Peter after the resurrection, John 21: 7–17:

> When Simon Peter heard that it was the Lord, he put on some clothes, for he was naked, and jumped into the sea. But the other disciples came in the boat, dragging the net full of fish, for they were not far from the land, only about a hundred yards off.
>
> When they had gone ashore, they saw a charcoal fire there, with fish on it, and bread. Jesus said to them, 'Bring some of the fish that you have just caught.' So Simon Peter went aboard and hauled the net ashore, full of large fish, a hundred and

fifty-three of them; and though there were so many, the net was not torn. Jesus said to them, 'Come and have breakfast.' Now none of the disciples dared to ask him, 'Who are you?' because they knew it was the Lord. Jesus came and took the bread and gave it to them, and did the same with the fish. This was now the third time that Jesus appeared to the disciples after he was raised from the dead.

When they had finished breakfast, Jesus said to Simon Peter, 'Simon son of John, do you love me more than these?' He said to him, 'Yes, Lord; you know that I love you.' Jesus said to him, 'Feed my lambs.' A second time he said to him, 'Simon son of John, do you love me?' He said to him, 'Yes, Lord; you know that I love you.' Jesus said to him, 'Tend my sheep.' He said to him the third time, 'Simon son of John, do you love me?' Peter felt hurt because he said to him the third time, 'Do you love me?' And he said to him, 'Lord, you know everything; you know that I love you.' Jesus said to him, 'Feed my sheep.'

- Try to imagine what Peter might be feeling in this encounter.
- Are there relationships that you wish you could restore, that seem lost for ever?
- Do you believe that you and others can truly change?

FURTHER READING ON JEAN VANIER AND L'ARCHE

Jean Vanier, *Becoming Human*, DLT, 1999.

Michael W. Higgins, *Jean Vanier: Logician of the Heart*, Liturgical Press, 2016.

Frances Young's theological engagement with her son's disability is also important: Frances Young, *Arthur's Call*, SPCK, 2014.

CONCLUSION: THE MERCIFUL HUMILITY OF GOD

Lent is an opportunity to stay close to Jesus. From the temptation in the wilderness, through his ministry, to its inevitable conclusion at the Cross, we walk through Lent, learning the ways of God made human. In Jesus, we are seeing what the life of God looks like in our human world, and so we are learning about the nature of our own reality, too. This is God's world: it came from God and returns to God, and although human beings have been invited into a way of living in the world that shapes it profoundly, yet they do not have the power, ultimately, to dictate its purpose.

As we walk the way with Jesus, then, we are relearning the human vocation, called to live and work with God for our good and the good of all creation.

The human being that God becomes is 'filial', shaped above all else by relationship with God the Father. So, in the wilderness, Jesus rejects other descriptions of his vocation, in favour of this one overriding definition: Jesus is the Son of the Father. Jesus lives in the world as though this is the true definition of humanity: it will be connected with God as child to parent, with all the vulnerability and dependence, trust and likeness that that implies. Jesus' way of being in the world suggests that love is the main definition of God's power. The resurrection and Ascension confirm that this is not just a temporary state, inhabited only by God incarnate, but the true and lasting reality of God. God is for us, as a Father for children; God is with us, as a brother among siblings; the Holy Spirit renews this, in water, in bread, in wine, making human beings into 'the body of Christ', the pattern of life-giving human and divine interrelationship. Human beings are called to be 'filial', to live as sons and daughters, sisters and brothers to each other. We are called to choose this definition of ourselves, as Jesus did, and to allow it to shape all our actions and our being.

Jesus lives in vulnerability, from birth to death, opening himself to the joy and pain of acceptance and rejection, offering always the relationship that he has with the Father. The prayer that Jesus teaches us, 'Our Father', longs for the time when the children of God will be as visible on earth as they are in heaven.

Jesus does not choose to be safe and protected, because that is not an option for love, as Jean Vanier has so clearly shown. Jesus does not choose to be 'successful', if success is measured by our usual standards. He meets only a few people, some of whom he heals, some of whom he annoys, some of whom come to love him, and are broken-hearted when he dies. The people he connects with are not the history-makers but the ones on the margins of all the usual narratives of who shapes the world and how. Unsurprisingly, these people cannot protect him from the anger, fear and indifference of the powerful, and so Jesus is executed, consigned to the scrap heap of history, among those many idealists and revolutionaries who tried to suggest that the world could be different.

At every point, like any other human being, Jesus has choices. His connectedness to God does not take away the ordinary struggle to decide, as we see in the test in the wilderness and the Garden of Gethsemane: 'he learned obedience', Hebrews 5: 8 says. Jesus chose, daily, to be the Son of the Father, and that choice required him to give up other things. To choose one way to live is at the same time to deny other choices. Jesus chose to give up other freedoms in order to retain this overwhelming freedom to be the Son of the Father. Philippians 2: 7 says that he 'emptied himself', as though the Son leaves behind all other possibilities, so that he is entirely free for this one, entirely filled only with the desire to be and do what God needed of him. 'Emptying' may sound like a negative thing, but part of our Lent journey has been to 'empty' ourselves of the practices that fill our lives and refuse to make space for God to invite us into relationship. 'Emptying' is in preparation for 'filling', as we hear God saying to us: 'You are my beloved.'

It is the bitterest irony of all that in order to be always and only the Son of the Father, Jesus even has to be prepared to abandon that central relationship. On the Cross, Jesus cries out: 'My God, my God, why have you forsaken me?' The one thing that had sustained him all his life is also given up, in obedience. It is given up so that in our alienation and God-forsakenness, there, too, is the Son of the Father, calling us home. Jesus gives up his connectedness even to God so that he can stay connected with us, as the Father sent him to be.

Augustine famously described the Holy Spirit as 'the bond of love', so strong that it cannot be broken, even by forsakenness and death. The resurrection is the sheer, unimaginable power of the love between Father, Son and Holy Spirit that no force in existence can overcome. This love is the unbreakable reality. It needs no protection, no force, no other power. The greatest destructive power in the universe, death, cannot prevail against it. The love of God, Father, Son and Holy Spirit is truer and stronger than anything, and since death and destruction cannot unmake it, it is the future of every past. Jesus' human story should have ended at the Cross, but it did not: it becomes a story with an infinite future, inviting all stories into it, to find their unimaginable newness. We, too, are invited to become children of God, so that our lives, our stories, are joined to the unbreakable love of God, and can have unimaginable futures.

In the world as we know it, the way of love is always vulnerable and liable to defeat. It walks humbly, seeking the good of others, willing to be misunderstood and used. It walks mercifully, noting and serving the needs of others, widening the circle of human companionship to include those who lack the strength and the resources to make themselves noticed. It cannot be defeated, because it is the deepest reality of the world, and so it is always hopeful, springing up in the most unlikely places. It can be infinitely patient, because it knows that empires will crumble, tyrants will fall, abusers will age and die, but love will keep rising from the dead.

In Jesus, we see God's humility lived out in the world, not claiming power or prestige or approval or safety; and we come to discover that this is a mercy and a blessing for us. We no longer have to be measured by failure or success, and so to face the fact that we all fail. Perhaps those who never had any illusions about their own abilities find it easiest to accept the merciful humility of God, that notices them, makes space for them, draws them in as valued parts of the human story of being called into relationship with God. The wealthy, the powerful, the successful, may find this harder to understand, until they come up against something that they simply cannot control or overcome, such as their own mortality. There may be space in God's mercy even for the powerful, if they know that the true measure of their power, like Jesus', was how far it was used to give and receive true humanity from others.

This is what we see in Jesus, as we walk through Lent, watching his ways. In Matthew 11: 25–30, Jesus is meditating on the intimate knowledge that Father and Son have of one another, and he turns from that to issue this invitation: 'Come to me, all you that are weary and are carrying heavy burdens, and I will give you rest. Take my yoke upon you, and learn from me; for I am gentle and humble in heart, and you will find rest for your souls. For my yoke is easy, and my burden is light.'

Jesus' 'yoke' is the one he chose consistently in his life, which is to be defined by relationship to God. All the other 'heavy burdens' of living up to other demands can be put down, under this yoke. That is why to serve God is perfect freedom.

Our Lent has given us the opportunity to trace God's strange ways in the world, and to notice how they make space for unlikely people, give voice to the unheard, confront the powerful with the limits of their control. For 40 days, we have been trying to see the world as God sees it, through the eyes of Jesus. We have tried to deepen our trust that God's 'foolishness' is greater than our 'wisdom', so that we can safely abandon our control and allow God to be God. Lent ends with Holy Week, Cross and Resurrection, and after that, the life of the children of God begins. We are sent out to practise merciful humility, as sisters and brothers of the Son. God stoops to make the earth home, the Son 'empties himself' to fill us with life. There is no place where God cannot be found, peacefully working an unimaginable future, with the humble and merciful power of resurrection life.

A NOTE ON THE AUTHOR

Dr Jane Williams is Assistant Dean and Lecturer in Systematic Theology at St Mellitus College. She is the author of several books, including *Approaching Easter* and *Approaching Christmas, Perfect Freedom, Who Do You Say That I Am?, Angels, Faces of Christ* and, most recently, *Why Did Jesus Have to Die?*